me
Hijra

me
Laxmi

Me Hijra, Me Laxmi

Laxminarayan Tripathi

Translated from the Marathi original by
R. Raj Rao and P.G. Joshi

OXFORD
UNIVERSITY PRESS

OXFORD
UNIVERSITY PRESS

Oxford University Press is a department of the University of Oxford.
It furthers the University's objective of excellence in research, scholarship,
and education by publishing worldwide. Oxford is a registered trademark of
Oxford University Press in the UK and in certain other countries

Published in India by
Oxford University Press
22 Workspace, 2nd Floor, 1/22 Asaf Ali Road, New Delhi 110002, India

© Oxford University Press 2015

The moral rights of the authors have been asserted

First Edition published in 2015
12th impression 2023

All rights reserved. No part of this publication may be reproduced, stored in
a retrieval system, or transmitted, in any form or by any means, without the
prior permission in writing of Oxford University Press, or as expressly permitted
by law, by licence, or under terms agreed with the appropriate reprographics
rights organization. Enquiries concerning reproduction outside the scope of the
above should be sent to the Rights Department, Oxford University Press, at the
address above

You must not circulate this work in any other form
and you must impose this same condition on any acquirer

ISBN-13: 978-0-19-945826-4
ISBN-10: 0-19-945826-X

Typeset in Goudy Oldstyle Std 11.5/17
by Sai Graphic Design, New Delhi 110 055
Printed in India by Manipal Technologies Limited, Manipal

All photographs are from Laxmi's personal collection unless
specifiedotherwise.

To my beloved parents
who have been my guiding light through the
highs and lows of my existence.
For standing by and making Laxmi who she is today.

Contents

Contents

One

Many great people have written great things about their childhood. There are so many moving poems about childhood. The sweet memories of childhood enrapture everyone. But not me. I'm different because I did not have a happy childhood. Parents love children and give them what they want. I, too, was given everything by my parents, and to this day there is nothing that I lack. But what I've never had is the innocence that makes a child what it is. I don't know what innocence is. If I tax my memory and try to remember the things of the past, all I can think of is illness, and ...

But, oh yes, I have some interesting memories of childhood too.

We lived in a shanty on the banks of the Siddheshwar Lake in Thane, Mumbai—mother, father, my older sister

Mintu (her real name is Rukmini), and myself. The house was tiny, and so was I. My name was Laxminarayan, and I also had an alias, Raju. As the only son of my parents (at that point), I was their favourite. I slept in my mother's arms.

In time, my younger brother Shashinarayan was born. Now, Shashi slept in mother's arms, while I slept in Papa's. I hated this. I fretted and fumed. Finally, one night when I could take it no longer, I wriggled free from Papa's arms and went to mother's bed. But the bed didn't have enough room for me—I fell off it in the middle of the night. Just below the bed was an aluminium bucket filled with water. The sharp edges of its mouth cut my leg. Despite the pain, I loved the way the accident made everyone fuss around me. I still have the bruise caused by the bucket on my skin, though it now lies concealed beneath a tattoo.

I recall an incident that happened in school. I was in kindergarten then. For the annual social gathering of the school, we had to enact the play *The Cap Seller and the Monkeys* on stage. I was the cap seller. Midway through the performance, my lungi came off—these days they call it wardrobe malfunction. The audience began to giggle with laughter. I was flabbergasted. I did not know what to do. I picked up my lungi and ran backstage.

Except for a couple of such hilarious episodes, my childhood was mostly fraught with illness. I had asthma from early on, and still suffer from it. Because I was sickly, I was well looked after in childhood. During periods of temporary recovery, I was subject to a host of restrictions—don't play here, don't go there, don't eat this, don't drink that. I was bored stiff. By the time I was seven, I had them all—typhoid, pneumonia, malaria, sometimes at one and the same time. Doctors, hospitals, medicines, injections, saline—these were my companions. There came a stage when the doctors gave up on me, believing my condition to be incurable. But it was the love of my parents that brought me back to life. Though my mother gave birth to seven children, only three of us survived, and she loved us more than she loved life.

Every time I recovered from illness, I was weaker than before. The restrictions imposed on me became even more rigid. My sister constantly kept a watchful eye on me. Was I playing in the dust? Was I eating trash? Was I taking the rest needed to recuperate? And so on.

I did not play with the boys of my age. Unlike them, I did not roam the mean streets or loll around in the mud. Although there was no dearth of friends around me, I started to live an internal life, the life of a loner.

My fragile health, however, did not prove a damper to my love for dance. I love dancing. In childhood, Bollywood songs invariably set my feet dancing to their tune. As a result, in school I was always selected by my teachers to perform on stage. The stage had a hypnotic effect on me. Once on it, I would forget who I was and danced to a frenzy. Nothing, not even my chronic breathlessness and cough, acted as a deterrent. I thus came to regard the stage as an oasis in the desert of ill health.

But my flamboyance on stage made some people uncomfortable. In patriarchal, misogynistic cultures such as ours, dancing is seen as a womanly pursuit. So I was teased. People began to call me a homo and a *chakka*. They couldn't see the cathartic and therapeutic effect that my art had on me. All they could see was that though I was a man, my body language was that of a woman.

Yes, it is true that I was like a woman. My mannerisms, my walking and talking style were all feminine. But why was it so? I did not know. I wasn't of the age to answer this question. Loner that I already was, I drifted even further into my cocoon.

Occasionally, I peeped out of my shell and opened up to a few trusted friends. These were my classmates—both girls and boys who were with me at school. Then there was my cousin Vijaypratap, whom we affectionately called Dadibhaiya because he kept a beard. He lived with us and was much older than us. But he loved us dearly and we thought of him as our eldest brother. At times he escorted us to school and brought our tiffin boxes to us at lunchtime. He also helped mother with the household chores. In my sickbed, I chattered with him non-stop. His job was to give me my medicines at the right time, skipping not a dose.

When Dadibhaiya got married, his wife Chaya also came to live with us. Soon, they had a daughter, Sonu. She was such a bubbly and healthy child, a veritable toy to us. We teased and pampered her. My brother Shashi, an ace prankster, would throw her up in the air and let her gently tumble to the ground, sending us in splits as that roly-poly of a baby landed on the floor.

Then tragedy struck. Dadibhaiya contracted jaundice and died of the disease. How I cried when he died. Dadibhaiya was so compassionate. No one understood me as well as he did. To me, personally, the loss was irreparable.

I was first sexually exploited when I was seven.

I had just recovered from yet another bout of illness and gone to my hometown for my cousin's wedding. I carried all my medicines with me. My family was around, and so were other relatives, for Indian weddings, as we know, are gala affairs accompanied by much hubbub and fanfare. The house was overcrowded. The adults went about their business, attending to this and that, while we children romped around. As we played, an older boy, a sort of distant cousin, lured me into a dark room and …

I was too young to understand that he was molesting me. Besides, my illness and the medicines I took made me feel weak and drowsy. Thus, I did not resist. But when the guy penetrated me, the pain was so excruciating I almost passed out. I have a hazy memory of all this. I remember that when I finally managed to rise, the fellow warned me not to report what had happened.

Sickly as I was, I had learnt to endure. I did not tell anyone about the ugly incident. Perhaps the guy's threats scared me. But a few days later, he molested me again, and then again. He was accompanied by his friends and all of them took turns to violate me. The physical and mental torture I went through is indescribable. But I didn't say a word to anyone, either then or later. I kept my feelings bottled.

After the wedding, we returned to Thane. But my sexual exploitation did not end. During family functions, when the whole clan got together, I was routinely molested by older cousins and their accomplices. It was as if my body did not belong to me but to them. They obviously derived a sadistic thrill from my suffering. But who would believe me if I complained?

These sexual assaults transformed me. I became secretive and incommunicative, hiding my feelings from my family and friends. Suddenly, it felt as if my childhood was over and I had grown up before my time.

Shashi, my brother, was also growing up. But he was my exact opposite. He was garrulous and mischievous, playing with all the older boys. Shashi was everyone's darling. Everyone pampered him. But his lifestyle terrified me. What if he took to bad company and went astray? I started keeping a watchful eye on him. After all, he was my kid brother. I started to follow him and take note of who he hung out with. Somehow, I came to the strange conclusion that the only way to prevent Shashi from going astray, was to let his friends have sex with me. And, the torture of anal sex notwithstanding, sometimes it was I who took the initiative to lure them into bed.

But for how long could I go on like that? I was doing things against my will. I was confused. There was agony in what we did, but there was also ecstasy. Today, in retrospect, I can understand my feelings a little better, but not at that time when I was a mere child. In time, I got fed up with the life I lived. I began to have my own opinions. I avoided sex. If someone tried to seduce me, I resisted it, first mildly, but then firmly.

The first time I refused to have sex with Shashi's friends, they were upset and angry. They cajoled me into acquiescing, and when that did not work, they blackmailed me. The blackmail scared me and I surrendered. The next time I got a little bolder and did not kowtow to their threats. They then got together and raped me. Enraged, I decided to speak to them in their own language. I decided to be as rowdy and aggressive as they were. I dared them to touch me. It worked. The boys put their tails between their legs, so to speak, and slipped away.

I discovered that passivity did not pay. It might endear me to society, but it came with a price. I decided at that moment to raise my voice against the things I did not like. Henceforth, I would not do anything against my will.

Two

 $\mathcal{M}$ aturity came to me early—at an age when most boys still go about in shorts and make a nuisance of themselves. I was now beyond my age and it was suffering that had made me so. I started hanging around not with the boys of my age, but with those who were older and wiser, irrespective of their gender.

Sangita Sethi was one such friend I had. She lived close by, and I called her Sangita auntie. Sophisticated in appearance, Sangita was affectionate. We got along very well. She was modern in outlook and spoke fluent English. Sangita encouraged me to participate in elocution competitions at school. She prepared me for these and I won prizes. The preparation consisted of her correcting my faulty grammar and making my vocabulary 'high level'. Whatever English I know today is because of

Sangita. The credit goes entirely to her. When Sangita and I chatted, it wasn't mere gossip. Instead, we discussed serious subjects like art, culture, history, dance, and even sexuality. Although I had gotten rid of the unwanted attention I received from Shashi's *tapori* friends and such like, I now myself began feeling attracted to boys in general. While I did not want some boys anywhere near me, I was attracted to others and strongly desired them. I wondered if this happened because inwardly I was a woman. I did not know. I was only in the fourth standard then. How was I to know? I discussed this with Sangita auntie. She patiently heard me out, and my feelings of bewilderment at my plight were replaced by solace.

One day Sangita auntie said to me, 'There is a person by the name of Mr Ashok Row Kavi who works for men like you. They are called gays.' Sangita gave me information about Ashok Row Kavi and an article on him that was published in *The Times of India*. I read it, and as soon as my fourth standard exams were over, I went in search of Ashok Row Kavi. In those days, Ashok and his friends met at the Maheshwari Udyaan in Mumbai, where they discussed issues concerning the gay community. When I reached Maheshwari Udyaan, I spotted the group and felt much better. They were like me, effeminate men, and people probably called them 'homos' just as they called me. I approached the group and asked them, 'Who is Mr Ashok Row Kavi?' At this, Ashok came up to me, affectionately patted my back, and asked me what I wanted. I introduced myself to Ashok, telling him everything about me. He smiled when I told him I had just finished my fourth standard exams. But his presence was so comforting that I opened out my heart to him. I shared my experiences with him and got him to clarify my doubts.

'I am effeminate,' I began, 'and people tease me. I am also sexually attracted to men. Why am I not like everyone else? Am I abnormal?'

Ashok smiled and said, 'No, my child, you are not abnormal. You are absolutely normal. What is abnormal is the world around us. They simply don't understand us. But don't think of all that now. Now that you have come to us, together we shall find a way. Carry on with your life. You are far too young. Finish your studies, and don't give up dancing. Come to me after you pass your SSC exams and I will explain everything to you.'

I felt relieved. The thought that I was not the only one like this, but there were others too was elating. In Ashok's group was a man named Goda, alias Vijay Nair. He performed my 'haldi-kumkum'. He took a pinch of Maheshwari Udyaan dust, smeared it on my forehead, and said, 'Welcome to the gay community. You have become one of us.'

When I got home that day, I floated on air. I was not alone. I had met people who were my kind. They shared my sexual attraction for members of my own sex. My confidence rose. I learnt a new word, 'gay'. I learnt its meaning, learnt how it applied to people like me. I was gay, not abnormal.

When I came to standard five, we left our house on the banks of the Siddheshwar Lake, and went to a place called Khopat to live. This was a chawl. Gujarati families lived all around us. On one side was the family of Bai-Bappa, and on the other, that of Premji Boricha. I used to quarrel a lot with Premji's wife. Their eldest daughter, Luna, was of the same age as Shashi. They were often seen playing together, and then fighting. The elders never paid attention to the quarrels of children. When Premji and his wife went out, they left their baby Mithun with us. We were truly a family.

Our change of residence was followed by another significant change. I changed my school from Singhania High School to a school called Beam's Paradise, which was closer to our house. The atmosphere at Singhania High School was disciplined and affectionate. Teachers and students spoke only in English. There was Miss

Menon, our crafts teacher, who taught us dancing. I liked her very much. Once, during a concert, she gave me the role of Gautam Buddha. To make me look bald, she stuck a wet papad on my head. I envied Lord Buddha his peace, and wished I had some of it myself.

Then there was Priyanka Marwa who lived in Mulund. On her birthday, we had a party at her house. We went to her house straight from school, without telling our parents. The party went on till late at night and my parents grew anxious. When I finally got home, I was spanked.

There were other good teachers at the Singhania school, such as Ray Madam, Rao Sir, Kulkarni Sir, and Dixit Sir. From such a conducive academic atmosphere, I came to Beam's Paradise. I did not have a school uniform, and on the first day, went to class wearing white shorts and a tomato-red shirt. The boys at this school were from the lower strata of society. Even so, we formed a congenial group that comprised students like Guruprasad, Bhagirathi, and Falguni. My feelings of alienation disappeared. Then, in standard six, we were joined by Nasir. He was so handsome. He had a sturdy build and fair skin. I got boisterous in his company and uprooted the tether like a calf developing horns.

I had my first love affair in the new house at Khopat.

I was in the sixth standard. A new family came to live in the building opposite ours. They had a son, Rohan, who was fair, like Nasir, and had strikingly good looks. But he was older than me by a good eight years. Still, I fell in love with him. I cared for none. No longer was I plagued by doubt or by thoughts about being abnormal. On the contrary, I had become brazen, ready to declare to the world that I was gay. Rohan loved me too. Outwardly, we were *yaars* and were inseparable. But in private, we touched each other, we hugged and kissed. I melted. Our relationship blossomed. It wasn't a sexual relationship per se—this was more about love. But when the sex finally happened, it was rejuvenating. All my previous sexual encounters were imposed on me. They left me feeling scarred and bruised. With Rohan, I was having sex by choice for the first time in my life. Now, there was ecstasy, not agony.

But then someone cast an evil eye on our love.

Rohan's younger brother and his cousin began to get fresh with me. When Rohan got to know of this, he was furious. He warned his brother and his cousin to keep their hands off me. But they didn't heed his warnings. Somewhere deep down I had the feeling that Rohan wasn't being firm enough with his brothers. He was allowing them to use me, as everyone else had done so far. I began to doubt whether Rohan really loved me. These destructive thoughts tired me out, and I wanted to take revenge on the whole world.

At this critical moment, as my mind was in a whirl, Rohan fell in love with a girl. The girl lived in our own neighbourhood. I found myself being the messenger who passed on love notes between Rohan and his girlfriend. I began to feel used and, after much thought, confronted Rohan with these things. We had a big fight and the affair blew up in my face.

During that time, I also made friends with boys in other schools. I loved playing basketball with them. I joined the summer club of St John's School and was in the Proline team. No one in the team suspected that I was different from them. Most team members were Christians—the Christians are a community that excels in sports. I still remember some of their names—Aloysius and Michael and Gloria. I made friends with a girl named Audrie. Her boyfriend cared for me as if I were his younger brother. I was pleased that at least some people thought of me as their own. Soon my asthma worsened and I began to tire very quickly. So I gave up playing basketball, though I continued to feel a part of this group of sportsmen.

Then there was a boy named Rahul Kale. I was introduced to him at a party in Koliwada, Thane. He was womanly like me and got teased often—even I couldn't resist teasing him. But our effeminate ways brought us together and we became friends. I admired Rahul's in-your-face approach to sexuality and imitated him. Together, we wandered the streets of Thane and went to parties. A while later, another guy, Mohan, joined us and we became a happy trio. We were the Madonnas of sexuality in Thane. Rahul went to a convent school, and in his company my English grew quite hi-fi.

But another yaar of mine, Pravin, did not like Rahul at all. He warned me not to get too close to him. 'He isn't a good guy,' Pravin often admonished me, though I did not agree with him. The truth was that Rahul, Mohan, and I were having one hell of a gala time.

Eventually, however, Pravin's words turned out to be true. Rahul had a bad habit of borrowing money from people to throw parties, but the money was never returned. I had an inkling of this, but did not make much of it. But as time went by, more and more skeletons tumbled out of Rahul's cupboard. I got to know that he swindled people, sometimes at knifepoint. I terminated my friendship with Rahul, though I never gave up the boldness I had acquired in his company.

Around this time, we went on a school trip to Matheran, a picturesque hill station close to Bombay. At night, Guruprasad, Nasir, and I slept on adjacent beds and it happened. Of course, I wanted it too, for I fancied Nasir. After Rohan, this was the first time I was enjoying sex. Yet, one thought rankled through my mind. I was a male. Then what was it about my body that attracted other men to me? Why was it always men who were turned on by me and never women?

Nasir and I became lovers. Or, it would be more correct to say that he was my protector. If anyone teased me in school, Nasir reported them to our class teacher. But if I was teased outside school, the culprits had it. Nasir, strongman that he was, beat them black and blue.

Besides being in the same school, Nasir and I also went to the same coaching class. The coaching class was on the road to a place called Robodi. Nasir's house was situated on this road. Indian towns are known for their *nukkad* culture. Nasir and his friends hung out at a *naka* close to his place. Some of them were Asgar, Zuber, Sufiyan, and Naved—all Muslims like Nasir. Nasir's friends became my friends too, and they never teased me. On the contrary, if anyone in the area bullied me, they came to my rescue. As Nasir and his yaars were thought to be the dadas of the area, no one dared to rag me. I spent a lot of time in the company of these boys, both on my way to the coaching class and when returning from it. Sometimes I bunked class just to spend time with the blokes. Truth to tell, I was in love with one of Nasir's friends, Sufiyan. But I did not have the courage to confess my love to him. What if he wasn't inclined that way? Besides, I was in a relationship with Nasir and decided to be faithful to him.

But then I met Ravi.

Though I lived in Khopat, which is in western Thane, my school was in Thane east. I went to school by public bus, boarding it at the Pratap Talkies bus stop. What was more; it was the same bus that came to the stop at the same time every day. Even the driver and conductor were the same. I had a favourite seat on the bus—the one next to the door. And since I boarded the bus at the starting point, I always got my preferred seat.

One day I hopped onto the bus and sat down on my earmarked seat. A guy entered and sat on the seat just behind me. After a while, he said to me, 'Is the seat next to you empty? May I shift there?'

'Please do,' I replied, looking at him intently. The guy stepped forward and sat down next to me. Then he extended his hand, saying 'Rakesh Jaiswal'. I shook his hand and let it remain there for more than the usual time. We became buddies there and then on that bus.

Rakesh had a circle of friends who lived close to the Jagmata temple at Kolbad. Their names were Nilesh, Brijesh, Sajish, Balu, Clifford, and Ravi. As in the case of Nasir's friends, the very names of these boys excited me. And, as in the case of Nasir's friends, I became the friend of all of Rakesh's friends, too. Like the former set, the latter, too, formed a protective cordon around me. Their policy was: no one dare say anything nasty or brutish to Laxmi. At the time, I was still a schoolboy, while my newfound friends were older than me by several years. Some of them had finished school or college and had started working. Ravi was one such working member of the group who had a job. Talking to him, looking into his eyes, I just fell in love with him, head over heels. My readers may think of me as sluttish. It is true that I had fallen in love with Rohan and Nasir earlier, but with Ravi it was different. My love for Ravi was characterized by restlessness as well as by solace. I started to keep a diary. If I did not meet Ravi at least once during the day, I would be uneasy, and the unease would be reflected in my diary entries. Ravi permeated my being to such an extent that day and night I could think of nothing and no one except him. I couldn't eat, drink, or sleep until I'd met him. On days when we did not meet, I sobbed like a small child. When he fell ill, I would carry food to his sickbed, sit by his bedside, and nurse him back to health. Pravin, as usual, cautioned me. 'The *banda* does not love you,' he said. 'He's merely being polite by befriending you. Don't be that involved with him.' These, of course, were words I did not want to hear.

My involvement with Ravi made Nasir jealous. He realized that though he was my friend and lover, my feelings for Ravi were more intense than for him. I had given over my soul to Ravi. This was unacceptable to Nasir, who thought of me as his 'girlfriend'. But I could do nothing to appease Nasir, for I was completely smitten by Ravi.

Then one day, I began to see a danger signal. I realized that Ravi was no different from the other boys with whom I'd had relationships, for, like them, he was after my body. He did not want my mind or my soul. I ruminated on the future of our relationship and came to the conclusion that it was bleak. For, society would never allow Ravi to 'marry' me or live with me even if he wanted to. Such relationships may be okay in the West, but not in India which is conservative. By being with Ravi, was I contributing to his downfall?

I arrived at a strange conclusion. I decided that if Ravi couldn't marry me, I would get him married to a girl who would love him throughout his life. I initiated steps to arrange Ravi's marriage and settle him down, after which I would walk out of his life. This may seem melodramatic now, but that's not how I saw it at that time.

Luckily for me, I had a close friend, Nisha, who liked Ravi very much. Nay, she loved him. To get Ravi to agree to tie the knot with Nisha, I played a trick on him. I introduced Ravi to Nisha's sister. They soon became friends, and Nisha was a frequent visitor to Ravi's home. Before long, Ravi fell in love with Nisha, everything going according to plan. I was happy, for the plan was after all architected by me, and I found myself voyeuristically enjoying their courtship.

But then I am human too. For a time, I was troubled by feelings of pain and jealousy. It was as if I had voluntarily built my own coffin. I calmed myself down and patiently waited for the marriage to take place. Once it was over, I walked out of Ravi's life forever. Today, Ravi and Nisha are a happily married couple. They have a cute son, Akash. As for me, my heart still palpitates when I set eyes on Ravi. It was calf love and I cannot get it out of my system.

On paper, I have dealt with my love affair with Ravi in just a few sentences. In reality, it was the catalyst that set me on a long, introspective journey. Does anybody fix the marriage of his own lover? Perhaps, it happens only in Bollywood films of the *qurbani* variety. Yet, that is exactly what I had done. This brought me to the question of sexuality. I had learnt from Ashok Row Kavi that I wasn't abnormal. But then, what was going on inside my body? Though I was born as a boy, how come I fell in love with boys and not with girls? Slowly, gradually, I came to the conclusion that I wasn't a boy. I was a girl. But then I had a penis and testicles, not breasts. So how could I call myself a girl? I was bewildered. I did not have the answers to these difficult questions. I wanted to end my life.

Three

*D*ancing saved me. It was the therapy I hadn't given up, in spite of going through turbulent times. In a way, it was my dancing, complete with my feminine movements of the waist, that contributed to my being thought of as effeminate. But I didn't care. I couldn't care less when I was younger, and I couldn't care less now. I began to take lessons in dancing from a professional dance teacher. Miss Menon, my teacher at Singhania school, was right. Dancing transported me to another world where I could be my true self. Everything else paled into insignificance when I was on stage, performing. My very first dance teacher was my own sister, Rukmini. She taught me to dance to the tune of Bollywood songs. Miss Menon came after her and brought finesse to my movements. In Beam's Paradise school, a teacher who was not a part of the regular faculty was especially invited to teach us dancing. Her name was Baby Johnny and she was a Malayalee Christian. She was cultured and beautiful. She would drape her *navvari* (nine-yard) sari around her waist so elegantly, with every fold right in place. She wore her hair long, had a big bindi on her forehead, and in the pendant of her ornate *mangalsutra* was a picture of her husband. A smile was perpetually planted on Baby Johnny's face. I regard her as the ladder that helped me climb to the peaks of fame as a dancer. It was she who gave me my first break as a dancer in school performances, together with other students like Zahida, Falguni, and Bhagirathi. In the company of these girls, I figured out that dancing was the oxygen that made me forget my ailments.

After school, I joined Baby Johnny's professional dance classes. I loved some of the things she said to us on the first day. For example, she often said that a sweeper should be like a sweeper, a doctor should be like a doctor, and a dancer should be like a dancer—both on and off stage. Baby Johnny believed that a dancer's movements must always be graceful, even when she is walking on the street. These words of Baby Johnny had a profound impact on me. They are deeply engraved in my mind. So much so, that when I became a hijra, I started to drape my sari exactly the way Baby Johnny did. I started to walk and talk like her. Today, everyone compliments me on my attire and on my personality in general. But the credit for it must go to Baby Johnny.

Baby Johnny also taught me other lessons in life. She taught me how to be myself, without compromising on my dignity and self-respect. She herself had lost her husband at an early age, and for mainstream society she was a widow. But she never wore her widowhood on her sleeve. Her hubby's memory was enshrined for her in her mangalsutra and that was that. She went about her daily routine with poise, conducting her dance classes, and mingling with her students. The one thing that I learnt from Baby Johnny was that in order to be respected by others, one had to first respect oneself. It seems to me that a lot of gays, lesbians, bisexuals, and transgendered people don't know this.

Inspired by Baby Johnny, I started my own dance classes. People acknowledged my dancing talent and sent their sons and daughters to me. I realized I had a flair for teaching, and the kids I trained were happy with the way I taught them. By the time I was in the eighth standard, my dance class was well established. I called it Vidya Nritya Niketan in deference to my mother, whose name was Vidyawati. Some of my star students were girls like Rachita Sethi and Flavia. Now, apart from teaching at my own class, I also went to other schools to teach. I loved winning prizes, for they gave my self-esteem a boost. Thus, I enrolled my name for whatever dance competitions I got to know of.

At one such inter-school dance competition, there was an incident that has stayed with me for life. I was to dance to the song 'Ye Birah Dasha' (This State of Separation) from the film Mohini. Competing with me was a girl who danced to the song 'Mera Assi Kali ka Lehanga' (My Petticoat with Eighty Pleats). I performed well and got applauded. But I was worried that it would be she and not me who won the prize. As it turned out, her audio-cassette let her down by refusing to work at the last minute. The girl began to weep on stage, and I was thrilled that the prize would now be mine for sure. I won the prize, but then the sad expression that I saw on the girl's face as I collected my prize told me that I had no right to it, for an injustice had been done to the poor thing. The incident, although relatively minor, made me hypersensitive towards injustice. Today, I have extra-sharp sensors to detect an injustice wherever I see it.

From Baby Johnny's classes, I graduated to classes run by Madam Vaishali who taught me how to dance Bollywood style. Later, I learnt bharatnatyam from teachers like Mahalingam and Vasant Kumar Pillay. My own students were now being invited to participate in high-profile TV shows like *Boogie Woogie*, anchored by the Jaffrey brothers, Javed and Naved, while I was invited to be a part of the audience. It was the first time I was on television. There was never a dull moment.

Dancing was my vocation, and I was fortunate to meet people who were on the same wavelength as I. One such guy was Deepak Salvi, introduced to me by my friend Sachin Kharat. Deepak became my business partner at Vidya Nritya Niketan. As time passed, we expanded operations and gave the school a new name. Today, we call the school Lucky Chap Dance Academy, and Deepak manages it full time.

But all was not hunky-dory. I may have been an ace dancer, but then I was a man, and dancing feminized my body. I was self-conscious about this, and my resolve to be bold and aggressive in the face of taunts and jibes did not stand me in good stead. My body was a playhouse and a plaything, and any man could do anything with it. Twice, I was almost raped, but managed to free myself from the clutches of my tormentors at the last minute. The first time, a gang of boys abducted me and took me to a thickly wooded area in Thane with the intention of outraging my modesty. But then something distracted them, and they fled towards the main road, leaving me naked in that jungle. The second time, I was all but raped in a room in which I had been locked up when I went to teach dance to a group of teenage boys.

Male-dominated society nauseated me. I realized that I would have to put up a lifelong fight to resist male lust. But how could I take on the whole world? As if to endorse how powerless I was, I was raped again. This time fourteen young men shut me up in a room and forced themselves on me. Then, a fifteenth man, unrelated to the fourteen, emerged from nowhere and saved me. I managed to scram for my life. The deeds of the Good Samaritan, however, made me see that it was wrong to paint all men with the same brush.

Love is a strange emotion. It has both bright and dark sides. In my case, the bright side was the love I got from my parents, teachers, and friends. The dark side was lust, which made me a victim of sexual assault again and again. My vulnerability made me worry about my brother Shashi whom I wished to protect at all costs. But unlike me, Shashi was masculine and this was the weapon that would save him from harm, come what may.

Things got so bad, that the mere touch of a man sent creeps down my flesh. I screamed if a man tried to make any sort of physical contact with me.

The gays of Maheshwari Udyaan provided solace, but then they saw themselves as men. That alienated me from them. I wondered why they did not regard themselves as women, for, to me, then, being homosexual and being a woman meant the same thing. Perhaps, it was the unconscious desire to be heterosexual, but when I was attracted to a man, I did not think of myself as a man. I thought of myself as a woman. That is why I became a drag queen, donning women's clothes and dancing at parties. My parents knew none of this, and are sure to have thrown me out of the house if they got wind of what I was up to. Fortunately, I had many alibis, like being a dance master, and, at the end of the day, this is what came to my rescue.

Amidst all the confusion, I managed to pass my SSC exams with 65 per cent marks.

Four

ME HIJRA, ME LAXMI

By the time I passed my SSC exams and joined Mithibai College in north-west Mumbai, I had become a riotous figure, carefree though not careless. It was as if cutting classes at college was my birthright. Mithibai College, located at an upmarket suburb of Mumbai (the Juhu–Vile Parle scheme) where the affluent live, was a highly fashionable place. Its ambience rubbed off on me and I became fashionable too. I also started to wear my sexuality on my sleeve. I usually went to college in men's clothes, for I was still a man, but sometimes I picked up courage and landed on campus in female attire. At such times, I made it a point to wear my favourite dark-coloured lipstick, Personi 113. I grew my fingernails long and wore small rings on various parts of my body. I was having a good time, and, surprisingly, no one sniggered at me. Perhaps, it had to do with the devil-may-care ethos of Mithibai College—anyone could do anything here. There were pubs around the college where song and dance parties went on all the time. I would be seen more at these parties than in the classroom.

I had already been a dance teacher since my school days. Now I became a model-coordinator who sent girls from my dance class to play bit-parts in Bollywood films. It was Anabel, a model herself, who introduced me to the work of model-coordination. When she saw me at the shoot of a music album by Kinu Ghosh, where I'd gone with two dancers Aarti and Ashwini, she approached me and asked me if I was a fashion designer. What gave her this impression was the way I was dressed. I had coloured my hair golden (this was at a time when hair colour had not even arrived in India), wore nose rings, and rings on my fingernails. Not the one to look a gift horse in the mouth, I told Anabel that though I wasn't a fashion designer, I ran a dance class and could provide her with fashion models. She agreed, and that is how I became a model-coordinator.

Anabel and I became close friends. She was going through a painful divorce at the time and the experience was traumatic. She confided in me and I comforted her, although, given the identity crisis I was experiencing, I needed to be comforted myself. May be it is the down-and-out who understand each other best. Anabel and I remain buddies to this day.

From supplying fashion models to Anabel, I graduated to providing models for films, television, and music albums. Sometimes, instead of giving away a part to other girls, I took it on myself because it gave me the opportunity to perform at various places in the state of Maharashtra, and it gave me a chance to travel. I was trying very hard to establish myself as an artist.

I got my big break when Vaishali Samant was shooting for her album *Lavani on Fire*. The dancers I sent her couldn't handle the intricate steps of *lavani*, a complicated dance form with a distinctly rural Maharashtrian flavour and with sexual overtones. Suddenly, Vaishali said to me, 'Why don't you dance yourself? You are way better than anyone else.' I was flattered. I put on make-up and commenced the shoot. The steps came to me so naturally. When *Lavani on Fire* was released, it was a runaway hit. I became famous as a dancer. People had already seen me on TV, but only as a member of the audience in shows like *Boogie Woogie*. Now, it was I who was the star and they came up to me for my autograph.

I noticed that in the world of glamour, no one looked at me with a curious eye, as they did in the world outside. Artistic people are actually supposed to possess angularities that mark them out from the run-of-the-mill. I, thus, wanted to be open about my sexuality and assert my sexual difference. This, of course, was easier said than done, for though I was proud of my quirks, I was also in need of social acceptance. Besides, I did not know where to turn as a sexual weirdo. The gay community of Ashok Row Kavi and his friends did not enchant me because they were co-opted by the everyday world. It seemed to me that they lived their lives and went about their business as heterosexuals do. This bored me. I liked being a drag queen. But then drag queens cross-dressed only sporadically, for shows, whereas I wanted to drape myself in a sari and wear skirts every single day.

My family didn't have an inkling of any of this. To them, I was Laxminarayan, the eldest son of the family, who went to college and had a job. They looked at me with hope. I was not just a son, but a dutiful son in their eyes, for I gave all my earnings to my mother to run the house. Not once was I asked how much I earned, how much I kept for myself, or what sort of work I did. It's not as if my folks didn't hear rumours about me—there were enough people around me to gossip. But unlike the folks of other hijras like, say, Revathi, they believed that everyone had the right to live as they wanted.

My next love was Jaspal, the friend of a friend. And I won him in a bet! I fancied Jaspal, confided in my friend, and he threw an open challenge before me. '*Patao* him and show me,' he said. I did. Don't ask me how. I guess by then I had irresistible charm. But what began as a joke took a serious turn as I fell madly in love with Jaspal. I began to live with him in a sort of live-in relationship. I did not go home to my parents for nights at a stretch. Nothing else was on my mind except Jaspal.

My business partner Deepak often said to me, 'Hey, man, stay away from Jaspal. He's not what you think. He's a hoodlum.' But was I in a mood to listen?

As in Ravi's case, and, indeed, in the case of everyone else who had come into my life so far, my love for Jaspal was one-sided. I loved him, but he did not love me. All he wanted was sex—ejaculation. And once he ejaculated, he did not think of me till he was horny again.

Eventually, Jaspal threw me out of his life. Of all my relationships, this one was the most traumatic. It hardened me for I resolved never to get emotionally involved with anyone again.

Through Ashok's circle of friends, I got to know a couple of hijras. One of them was Sweety, a bar dancer.

She introduced me to the world of bar dancing. 'You dance well, and the money's good,' she said to me matter-of-factly. She took me to a dance bar at Grant Road. I danced like a *tawaif* before an audience of sexually starved men, and made a large pile of dough. The bar had sleazy settings, but this was conducive to the kind of work one did there. With the money I made, I bought fashionable clothes and expensive make-up kits. I needed creature comforts. I was spoilt—I had acquired the habits of an aristocrat. I worked in the dance bar at Grant Road for a good four years and eleven months. During this time, I got addicted to money, earned it and squandered it.

But, of course, a dance bar is not just about dancing. It's also about sex. My clientele wanted sex, but this I never gave them, forbidding anyone to touch my body. If I did have sex, I made sure that it wasn't sex work. That is to say, I did not have sex in exchange of money. I have always considered myself to be monarch of my own body.

Dance bars have a flip side too. It was only when I worked in a dance bar that I saw for myself the deplorable conditions in which the women there lived. There was Deepa, there was Alisha. One had been raped by an uncle; the other had been traded to prostitution by her own brother. Yet others had found their way to the dance bar because they were battered and abandoned by their husbands. Some girls were from royal tawaif families that had fallen on bad days after Independence. When the government abolished the privy purses of the princes, these women lost their patronage. They began to starve. Mumbai's dance bars were their only option. But the tawaifs only danced. They did not do sex work. Because they were from pedigreed families, they were beautiful. Men went mad at the very sight of them: their beauty sent their heads spinning. But though the tawaifs did not do sex work, they made sure not to offend their customers by spurning them. It was a tight rope walk, this business of making every man in the bar feel you were in love with him, without actually being even remotely interested in the guy. It called for high histrionics.

Back home, the tawaifs and other bar dancers had parents and brothers and sisters and children to look after. After all, they did what they did only because they loved their families and couldn't bear to see them perish. In order to soothe their woes, the girls often took to drinking. Some of them became drunkards. Some even died of alcoholism.

And where was I in all this? How did I fit into such a scenario? True, I didn't have to support a family. But I, too, straddled many worlds, without belonging to any. As the eldest son of my parents, they expected me to be a man. They expected me to be manly, and eventually be the man of the house. I knew I couldn't fulfil these expectations because, inwardly, I did not feel like a man. On top of that, I was gay. Even if my parents overlooked my aberrations, society would not. I felt inadequate. I wanted to be addressed as a woman, not a man. I was in turmoil.

Like my dance-bar friends, I took to drinking. Drinking provided succour. A time came when I started to drink quite heavily.

I did not tell my folks that I worked in a dance bar. It would break their heart. To them, I was still a model-coordinator who studied at Mithibai College. We had by then moved out of Khopat and gone to live at Shastrinagar. I did not get home before two every night, and when my mother asked me where I had been, I lied, saying I was at a shoot or a party. It was also a question of family honour. We belong to a high-caste Brahman family from Uttar Pradesh, where girls don't even go out to work. To work in a dance bar would be the ultimate transgression. Yet, I wanted a lifestyle. I wanted to live like the rich and the famous. When mobile phones came to India, I was among the very first to buy an expensive handset.

Five

Gloria was a model for whom I coordinated. Late one evening, she called me on my mobile and said, 'Hey, Laxmi, my brother is like you, will you meet him?'

'Okay,' I said.

I arranged to meet Gloria's brother at the CST station the next day. After finishing some odd jobs in the Fort area, I strolled to the station and met Lawrence Francis, alias Shabina. Shabina was a hijra. She was dressed in a sari. She looked every bit a woman from head to toe. Everything about her—her speech, her gait, her mannerisms, and her voice—was so feminine. I knew at that very moment that I yearned to be like Shabina. As soon as we introduced ourselves, I said to Shabina, as if I'd known her for years, 'Come, I'm hungry. Let's go to Café Mondegar and have something to eat.'

But Shabina was reluctant. She said, 'No, not now. We'll have something here itself.'

At first, I did not understand why Shabina made such a fuss. Then I realized it was because she was a hijra who faced bias and discrimination. I felt sorry for Shabina. I was also angry that she did not stand up for her rights. I made it a point to take Shabina to Café Mondegar that evening.

Shabina and I grew close. The feeling that I'd known her for ever persisted. I found Shabina work in the fashion world. Though the fashion world is full of queer and unconventional people, eyebrows were raised when I was seen with Shabina. Word got to my parents that I was hanging around with a hijra and my mother finally confronted me. I dismissed all that she heard as cheap gossip and set her at ease.

I learnt everything about hijras from Shabina. She acquainted me with their history, their traditions, their lifestyle, and their sources of income. She pointed out that the hijras had virtually no support system to safeguard their interests. I began to realize that the hijras were a culturally rich sub-sect. Not everyone could become a hijra—it took guts. The word '*hij*' refers to the soul, a holy soul. The body in which the holy soul resides is called 'hijra'. The individual is not important here.

What is important is the soul and the hijra community that possesses it. God loves the hijra community and has created a special place for it outside the man–woman frame. A hijra is neither a man nor a woman. She is feminine, but not a woman. He is masculine, a male by birth, but not a man either. A hijra's male body is a trap—not just to the hijra itself who suffocates within it, but to the world in general that wrongly assumes a hijra to be a man.

I had suffocated all along. I had been a victim of the wrongful assumptions of the world. Till I met Shabina and got the answers to all my questions. At school, history was my favourite subject. I now voraciously read everything I could lay my hands on about the hijras, and talked to many people. The more I thought about it, the more I was convinced. Yes, that was the answer. I was a woman and the world must see me as such.

I decided to become a hijra. But that is easier said than done. I often said to Shabina, 'When I become a hijra, you will be my guru.'

It's not as if I'd not met a hijra before. In Mumbai, there's a colony of hijras at Sonapur in Bhandup. Hijras like Mary and Manjula Amma lived there. I ran into them sometimes when I went for a performance, and always felt that I was on the same wavelength as them.

And now, the day had dawned at last when I wanted to be one of them.

Fate was on my side. Manjula Amma invited me to dance at a puja that was taking place at Sonapur, Bhandup. After my performance, someone came up to me and asked, 'Child, whose *chela* are you?'

'Shabina's,' I impetuously blurted out, and was surprised at my own guts. It was my unconscious self that spoke, making it abundantly clear to me that my desire to become a hijra was intense. Then what am I waiting for, I asked myself.

I rose and went to the Lucky Compound at Byculla. The heads of all the hijra gharanas lived there. I knew that the head of Shabina's Lashkar gharana lived on the second floor. Nervous, I reached the second floor. Lata Nayak [Shabina's guru] held court. There were many hijras around her. Most of them were over six feet tall and well built, and wore saris. I was conspicuous in my shirt and jeans. For a moment, the sight of the hijras terrified me. But they put me at ease. They served me water.

'What do you want, child?' one of them tenderly asked me.

I mustered the courage to say, 'I want to become a chela.' Then I awkwardly added, 'How much ... is the fee?'

My naivety amused the hijras. They burst out laughing. Lata Nayak said, 'No, child, there is no fee. If you really want to, you can become a chela.'

Then a very short ceremony took place. I was given two green saris, which is a ritual that takes place when one joins the community. They are known as *jogjanam* saris. I was crowned with the community dupatta. My *reet*, the christening ceremony, was thus performed and I became a hijra.

It was 1998.

Six

When I became a hijra, a great burden was lifted off my head. I felt relaxed. I was now neither a man nor a woman. I was a hijra. I had my own identity. No longer did I feel like an alien.

The day I became a chela at Byculla, I was sent to Lataguru who lived in Govandi, Mumbai. She was Shabina's guru. I had never been to Govandi before. It is on the harbour line that connects Mumbai to Navi Mumbai, and I was travelling on this route for the first time. It was also the first time that I set foot on Govandi. Hereafter, there would be many things that I would do for the first time in my life.

It took me a while to find Lataguru's house in that cluster of houses, but I finally got there. Lata Nayak had already called Lataguru from Byculla and informed her that she was sending her a chela. So Lataguru was expecting me. However, she knew nothing about me. As we chatted, we discovered that both of us came from the same part of Uttar Pradesh. I was happy, for this served to break the ice between us. We spoke in Hindi, though my Hindi was peppered with English words. Lataguru couldn't believe that a boy from a good family, who was college-educated and stylish, should opt to be a hijra.

I said to Lataguru, 'I live in a family with parents, a brother, and a sister. I wear shirts and trousers at home. I cannot afford to wear a sari.'

To this, she replied, 'For now, live with your family and carry on as usual. Continue to wear trousers and shirts. It's no fun wearing a sari, and nor is it compulsory to do so. Leave the two saris that you got as jogjanam here. When Shabina comes to meet me, do come along with her. I will tell you then what to do next.'

I felt relieved that I did not have to wear my hijrahood on my sleeve. I did not have to disclose my status as a hijra to anyone unless I wanted to. I touched Lataguru's feet and left.

I travelled to Cheeta Camp where many hijras lived. Priya, a friend of Shabina and mine, lived there. I announced to Priya that I had joined the community. She was so happy that she gave me a sari as a present. Then she told me about the organizational work that

Shabina and she jointly did for the DWS. We chatted till late and finally I got home.

I did not give a clue to my family about the transformation that had come about in my life. I behaved normally, wore my usual clothes. I wasn't ready to tell them anything yet. Nor did they suspect.

At the same time, I couldn't keep my secret all to myself. So I shared it with a couple of intimate friends who were shocked beyond belief. When they recovered, each one of them reacted differently. Some said, 'Why have you brought this hell upon yourself?' Others were so pissed that they stopped talking to me. But to Pravin, my boyhood buddy, it made no difference. He said, 'You were, you are, and you will always remain Laxmi for me.'

I was hurt by the attitude of my friends. But then it was expected, for I had chosen to swim against the current. In any case, I wasn't going to make an about turn.

Let alone my friends, even fellow-hijras were surprised by my transformation. To their way of thinking, only the wretched of the earth became hijras. A college-educated boy, who was an accomplished dancer and had the support of his parents, had no need to.

On my part, I wanted to understand the psyche of the hijra community. I observed them closely and made a mental note of how they behaved when they were by themselves, with their gurus, or in a group. It was mandatory for me to internalize this behaviour if I wanted to succeed. Gradually, I restricted my use of male clothing to the house and started to wear saris whenever I went out. People knew I wore saris when there was a performance and, in the beginning, I used that as an excuse, telling them I was headed to this or that show, or this or that rehearsal. But when they saw me in a sari all the time, they smelled a rat. 'How can there be shows thirty days a month?' they intriguingly asked me. Soon the news reached my parents, and then it happened ...

It was the turn of the century. There were protests against Section 377 of the Indian Penal Code all over India. Section 377 outlawed homosexuality, called it unnatural. A meeting was called at the Press Club in south Mumbai, and it was attended by Ashok Row Kavi as well as members of the hijra community. I was there too. After the meeting, television channels gheraoed us for bytes. Zee News channel wanted my byte as a hijra. Ashok cautioned me. 'If you appear on TV, your family will know that you are a hijra,' he said. 'If you think this will make life difficult for you, don't speak to them [the reporters].'

I was confused. But such was my desire to become a celebrity that I decided to appear on TV, come what may.

As soon as the cameras were switched off, I frantically called up Shashi at home. 'Don't turn on the TV,' I panted. 'Don't let Mom and Papa see the news.'

Shashi was perplexed. I briefly told him what had happened, but called him to Thane station to meet me and hear the rest.

When I met Shashi at Thane railway station, after a sixty-minute train ride from CST, he sulked. 'Why did you do this?' he screamed. 'Have you gone mad?'

In vain, I tried to calm Shashi down. I took him to a hotel near the station and told him everything from scratch. As we talked, I received a call on my mobile from my mother. 'What have you been up to?' she angrily asked. 'Come home at once. We want to talk to you.'

What will be, will be. Mom and Papa had gotten to know that I had become a hijra. It didn't matter who told them—the fact was that they knew. Shashi and I started for home. I prepared myself for battle.

As we entered the house, mother began to beat her breasts and wail loudly, as if there was a death in the family. Perhaps it was the most spontaneous way to react when confronted by the news that the scion of the family has become a hijra.

Someone brought my mother a glass of water. When she was able to speak, she said, 'No one in fourteen generations has done such a thing in our family. We are a noble, high-caste Brahman family. Didn't you think of our self-respect? Your sister is married. What will her husband's family think of us?'

The verbal diarrhoea went on for long. I quietly listened to their tirade. What else could I do? When they cooled down, they attempted to talk me out of what I had done. 'Why did you have to do this? Tell us what your problem is. Don't you have everything going for you? You are educated and are a famous dancer. Why don't you concentrate on dancing? We'll give you money to start a business. What you have done is so damaging that we will have to hang our heads in shame. But it's not good for you too. Please get it out of your system.'

I was harangued, but I patiently listened. I could empathize with my folks. I had shattered their hopes in me.

Historically, hijras are respected in Uttar Pradesh. They are called upon to bless newborn children and newly married couples. People believe that the blessings of a hijra come true. And the belief originates in no less a source than the Ramayana itself. It is said that when Lord Rama began his fourteen-year exile in the forests, the people of Ayodhya accompanied him to the outskirts of the town to bid him farewell. Here, Lord Rama turned to his subjects and said to them, 'Oh, all you men and women who love me, please return to your homes. I will complete my exile and be back among you.' Among his subjects were hijras too. They were neither men nor women. They couldn't go back to their homes, for he had implored only the men and women to return home. The hijras thus stayed put at the outskirts of the town for fourteen years until he returned. Lord Rama was moved by the penance of the hijras. He granted them a boon: their blessings and their curses would come true.

Be that as it may, it was naturally unacceptable to my parents that their own son should become a hijra. Supermen are okay as long they are born to others. No one wants supermen in their own homes. My parents wanted me to lead a normal life. They wanted me to get married and beget children. My grandfather, Harisharan Tiwari, was such an erudite scholar; he knew the Vedas and the Upanishads by heart. And I, his grandson, was a hijra! Now tongues would wag even more than before. My parents would scarcely be able to leave the house. They were torn between the demands of society and the love of their son. But how could I let them stifle me?

The next day our lives started as usual. We carried on with our activities without exchanging a word. My father did not speak to me. As for my mother, she cried non-stop for three whole days. Things came to a head when, in a fit of anger, she sheared off some of my hair. I could take it no longer. I drowned my sorrow by starting to work for the hijra community.

Seven

I now spent almost all my time with the hijras. I had learnt enough about them to write a book, so to speak, and I was proud to be a part of the community. I knew about Arjuna who had become Bruhannada in the Mahabharata, and I knew about the Khojas who guarded the harems of kings. I also knew about Shabnam Mausi, the MLA from Madhya Pradesh, who was the first among us to join politics.

Three weeks after I became a hijra, it was Muharram. The Tijja of Muharram holds great significance for us hijras. According to custom, ten hijras became my disciples and I performed their *chatai*. Some of them were Subhadra, Winnie, Sheeba, Rita, Harsha, and Neeta. Shabina's disciple Nikita wanted to be my disciple, too, but I made her my *gurubhai* instead. In time, my disciples had their disciples. I became a *nani*, then *parnani*. Subhadra was my senior-most disciple and was actually older than me. Her chelas were Tulsi, Rajashree, Karishma, Damini, Neeta, Shahin, Murgi, Kamal, Anju, and Muskaan—my family was growing rapidly. I was their guru, the head of a large family. All of them lived in a cattle shed near Kharegaon Lake. It was my *hijrakhana*. Some of these girls were bar dancers, others did sex work, and still others performed *badhai* at weddings and childbirths. Most of the action took place in a neighbourhood known as Sheelfata. On the other hand, I continued to live with my family. The anger of my parents was on the wane. We began speaking to each other. In our family, we are not the sort who nurse grouses for ever and ever. We are transparent—we openly tell one another what we like or dislike about them. Though I was a hijra now, I did not put an end to my other activities. My model-coordination work and dance classes continued. Sometimes I danced in a bar. It was situated in Ulhasnagar, and while returning from there, I would drop in at Sheelfata. I enjoyed the banter I had with the other hijras at Sheelfata. On the whole, life was good. I was proud that I was a hijra.

In our group, only Sangeeta, Mardana, and Vardaan did sex work. Soon the police began to harass them. There were bitter quarrels between the cops and the girls, and they landed up at the Sheelfata police station. Though these girls were not my chelas, they were hijras all the same, and the police had been brutal in their dealings with them. I followed the girls to the Sheelfata police station and raised a stink there. It helped being a hijra because the public often think of us as troublemakers and, given a choice, would avoid engaging with us. It was likewise with the cops. They finally released the girls and let them go home. The encounter with the police gave me an idea of the kind of life I would be leading in the years to come. It would be a life of social and political activism.

Subhadra, my senior-most chela, was my twin. She was a south Indian from Mangalore. We resembled each other strongly. Although Subhadra was older than me, she called me her guru. In the hijra community, being a guru has little to do with age. It has more to do with wisdom.

December came, and the hijras wanted to celebrate New Year's Eve at Vajreshwari. Though I wasn't keen on it, they insisted that I should accompany them. I had to comply. I returned from a show on the afternoon of the 31st and asked them to proceed to Vajreshwari, promising that I would follow. I kept my promise. Once there, we sang and danced and ate and drank till midnight. I had to catch a flight early next morning for a show in Hyderabad. But that didn't deter me. Before we parted, Subhadra pestered me to give her the dress I was wearing. It was brand new, but I ungrudgingly changed and handed it over to her.

On 2 January, Subhadra wore my new dress and went for sex work. She never returned. I rushed back from Hyderabad and filed a complaint at the local police station. Subhadra was missing. The police now came after us. They looked at us with suspicion and bias, subjecting us to questions and cross-questions. I urged the police not to think of us as hijras, but as human beings. I told them that if charges could be proved against any of us, we would voluntarily hand ourselves over to them. They conducted a thorough inquiry, assisted by us, hijras, but Subhadra was untraceable. What could have happened to her?

Subhadra's disappearance filled us with anxiety. Yet, life had to go on. A day passed, then two. I started offering my services to the DWS. It was early morning and I was getting ready to attend a DWS meeting when I got a call from the police station. Subhadra was dead. I was to reach the police station as soon as possible. But my meeting was important and I had to attend it. On the way, I called my lawyer to apprise him of the situation.

He advised me not to ask for possession of the body, as this could complicate matters. I, therefore, decided not to claim the body. The hijras were distraught. I told them not to weep. I advised them to switch on the radio to reduce their gloom. Uncertainty loomed large over us. Subhadra's death had opened our eyes to the dangers of being a hijra. But I had to put on a show of bravery before the others, for I was their guru. If I crumbled, what would become of them? At last, when we could bottle up our grief no longer, we went to the Kalwa Bridge and gave vent to our feelings. We broke down. We sobbed and hugged each other. It was night by then.

But how did Subhadra die? Clearly, Subhadra had been murdered. This meant that the case was transferred to the Crime Branch of the Thane Police. They directed their officers at the Mumbra Police Station to conduct an inquiry, and days of bureaucratic harassment followed. To be with the other hijras in their hour of crisis, I shifted to Kalwa. Prince that I am, I slept on a bare mat here for the first time in my life, but I did not mind it one bit. Trivialities ceased to matter to me anymore. What mattered was our sense of solidarity. That alone would save us.

The cops would arrive at the most unearthly hour and randomly pick anyone of us up for questioning at the police station. If we asked for details, we were given evasive answers, like 'someone told us ...' or 'our sources have revealed ...' But such responses did not satisfy us. We demanded that we have an audience with their informants, whoever they were. We also demanded that none of us be touched by them, for the police in India are known to beat up people or get fresh with them, especially if they are women, at the drop of a hat.

The stress and strain of all this told on my health. I was fatigued and was losing my morale. Our fight with the world seemed so very pointless. But we couldn't give up the fight either. The world would only be too happy to silence us. But we couldn't afford to be silenced. We couldn't afford to be thrown into jails and forgotten altogether.

I gave my chelas a crash course on hijra behaviour. I taught them how to face the cops, when to abuse, and when to be gentle, and I taught them many other things besides.

I now spent very little time with my family at home. One day, I had barely managed to get home after a long spell outside, when Murgi ran in after me and cried, 'Guru, the police have picked up Shaheen and Kekda.' As she spoke, she trembled with fear. I was enraged. My pleas to the police to behave themselves had fallen on deaf ears. I left for the police station at once, taking poor Murgi along with me.

I stormed into the inspector's cabin and gave him a bollocking. He capitulated, and Shaheen and Kekda were released.

Subhadra's assassins could never be found. The police shut the case for want of evidence. This was a big blow to us. A hijra's death, nay murder, didn't seem to matter to anyone. But it mattered to us, Subhadra's sisters, and we would go through it alone. I recalled Tagore's words: *Ekla chalo.*

Eight

Meanwhile, I rendered my services to the DWS. The *dai*'s main job was to take care of the hijras, especially those who had had their *nirvana* (castration). The DWS, in turn, protected the interest of the dais, bringing them into the organized sector. I had done social work before, but it mainly involved the distribution of condoms to hijras who did sex work for a living. These hijras were also prone to contracting sexually transmitted diseases and AIDS, and if a hijra was ill, we took her to the Sion Hospital, where I had established a rapport with Dr Hema Jayrajani.

Like any other community, the hijra community too has its conservative elements. The *nayaks* (leaders) are a case in point. They arbitrate against the use of condoms by hijras because condoms put off clients, and this deprives the hijras of their means of livelihood. Modern-day hijras, of course, buy none of this gibberish. They know that condoms can save them from deadly diseases like AIDS. Besides, their customers too have woken up to the need for safe sex. Thus, one sees long queues of hijras at the distribution centres, waiting for the tempo with the condoms to arrive.

While my social work kicked off, things again went down the ladder on the home front. My parents stopped talking to me, possibly because of the taunts my sister faced from her in-laws on my account. My sister's husband was a fighter pilot. He belonged to a profession that put a premium on manliness. How could he be expected to take kindly to me, who had jettisoned my manhood of my own accord? Shashi continued to wallow in shame. I discovered that the younger generation, made up of Shashi and my sister and brother-in-law, was more willing to talk, to have a dialogue with me, than my parents. My parents were so ill-informed about the matter that they thought that the cure for my madness was marriage. Accordingly, they started to look for a girl for me, purposely keeping me in the dark.

One day, Papa summoned me, made me sit by his side, and said, 'We've found a girl for you. She's from a good family and you must marry her.'

I was aghast. I told my father that I did not want to get married, and if I did, I would spoil not only my own life, but also that of my wife. After that, I would be left with no other option but to take my own life.

Tears gathered in my father's eyes. In my twenty-year life, this was the first time I saw him cry. I felt awful, for I knew my father loved me dearly. When I was a child, he indulged me always. As the head of the family, he could have easily thrown me out of the house when I became a hijra, but this he did not do. My mother never questioned me about my whereabouts even when I returned home in the wee hours. Instead, she waited at the door for me to serve me my dinner. And now, this was how I was repaying my parents for the love and affection they had showered on me.

I was on a guilt trip. I felt I had betrayed my parents. At the same time, I had to be faithful to myself. I was not born to be a man, and that was that. Was there a middle path? Could I both please my parents and be true to myself? I would achieve the former by fulfilling all my responsibilities as the eldest son of the family. (This, of course, wouldn't include marriage.) And I would achieve the latter by working indefatigably for my community.

I now gave top priority to DWS work. I became a peer educator who went to hijra colonies to educate the hijras about sexually transmitted diseases, including AIDS. Here, I learnt a lot from Shabina and Priya who were experienced social workers. Social service can be a bitter pill with adverse side effects. But I was determined to dedicate my life to social work.

Then, suddenly, Shabina and Priya left the DWS after differences of opinion with some of the society's members. Priya quit first, and later Shabina followed her. They went to Chennai. It was as if the entire hijra community in Mumbai had ganged up against them. But the loss, I believe, was the DWS's, for both Shabina and Priya were committed workers.

After their exit, Lataguru called me and said, 'So what shall we do now? Who will look after this voluminous work? I have no education and will not be able to run an organization about which I know next to nothing. But you are educated. If you agree to take on the responsibility of running the DWS, it will survive, or else it will close down.'

The DWS was doing great work and it saddened me to think that the society would have to close down. It was through the efforts of the DWS that hijras from the lowest strata of society, who either begged or did sex work to earn a living, came to be noticed. The DWS was the only group that made mainstream society aware of the indignities of being a hijra. It was truly a body of, for, and by the hijras. The rest of the world was hostile to hijras and saw them as a menace, the way rats and cockroaches are thought of as a menace. As far as health-related issues were concerned, the government's anti-AIDS programmes were hardly directed at the hijras. They were directed at women (prostitutes). Social work had respectability to it. It provided the much-needed antidote to the taunts and the ridicule that I otherwise faced. As a social worker, no one could treat me as a doormat. But I alone being respected wasn't enough. I wanted that respect to percolate down to the lowest of the low among the hijras, so that we were all treated on par. And this is where an organization like the DWS helped. It bolstered the confidence of the hijras and freed them of the slave mentality. So closing down the DWS wasn't an option.

I pondered the issue and said to Lataguru, 'I am ready to take up the responsibility of running the DWS. We mustn't think of closing it down at any cost.'

I thus became the first chairman of the DWS.

It is one thing being a peer educator, and quite another being a chairman. As chairman of the DWS, I now had to look after the welfare of the entire hijra community in Mumbai. I felt empowered, and empowerment is not a word that normally exists in the vocabulary of a hijra. It is true that as a person, I, Laxminarayan Tripathi, liked taking on new challenges, but as a hijra I was never allowed to.

My hour of fame came when, on behalf of the DWS, I was invited to a workshop on Proposal Development at the Avert Society in Vashi. I had to make a presentation, and I knew not the ABC of how presentations are made, though I knew the meaning of the word 'proposal'. I was assisted in my task by a friendly couple at the Avert Society, Sandip and Nidhi Dube. Gathering all physical, mental, and material resources at my command, I finally made the presentation in chaste, fluent English and got many claps for it.

Everyone was amazed. Their stereotypes about hijras were dismantled. The chiefs of many well-known organizations were present at the workshop, and one of them was my client at the dance bar where I worked. At first, he felt uneasy on seeing me in the auditorium, for I was associated with his nightlife. When I made my presentation, however, his tongue popped out, and he almost fell off his chair in disbelief.

After my success at the workshop, I decided to leave my disreputable past behind and assume a respectable persona. Accordingly, I stopped dancing at the dance bars. I refrained from going there even if I was tempted to. I grew articulate. I wanted to be a member of the talking classes. The word 'dialogue' was my watchword. Whoever it was that I was dealing with, be it a DWS hijra or a company chairman or a project funder, I wanted to have a dialogue with him. It was sheer theatre. As a dancer, I was a performer, and now I was performing here as well as delivering my lines and gauging the response of my audience. I loved what I was doing. After Avert, I made my next presentation at the Mumbai District AIDS Control Society (MDACS). And once again I left my audience speechless.

Work took me to Kamatipura, Mumbai's notorious red-light district. I could have gone there as a prostitute. Instead, I was going there as a delegate. It so happened that a team from Delhi had arrived to evaluate the work of the DWS and I was accompanying them. Not that I didn't know about Kamatipura. Zeenat, a hijra who lived here, used to visit us. She would talk of its many horrors. But this was theoretical knowledge. Now I was seeing the sordidness and the squalor with my own eyes. I was shocked.

The rooms in which the prostitutes lived and worked were veritable pigeonholes, devoid of air and light. But each pigeonhole was further partitioned off to accommodate multiple clients. A foul smell emanated from the rooms. In these conditions, the girls sold sex. This baffled me, for I always thought sex could only be pleasurable when the settings were pretty. Here was ugliness personified. One couldn't even move sideways! But the girls had gotten used to it, just as office clerks get used to the humdrum of their job. But clerks, at least, can go on strike. Did these girls even have the right to protest? It was slave labour at its worst.

I turned to look at the customers. One was bearded; another had a large gash on his forehead; yet another wore a turban. They came from all religions and were of all ages. Some of them hid their faces so as not to be identified. Others were more upfront, probably having lost all sense of shame. But all of them were hypocrites. They fucked prostitutes and then went back to wives and mothers and sons and daughters to be a part of the respectable society.

My head spun. The activist in me was stirred. I naively thought I could single-handedly change the system.

But could I, me who was infinitesimal? I decided to become one of them, the prostitutes of Kamatipura. Not to do sex work (though, perhaps, that too), but to have a dialogue with them. They wouldn't open up to anybody who wasn't one of them. I would change the system from within. I made frequent trips to Kamatipura from that day onwards.

Then came Mr R.R. Patil's puzzling announcement that all dance bars in Maharashtra would be closed. He was the home minister then. The dance bars, according to the honourable minister, corrupted our youth. But what about the women who worked at the dance bars who would starve? That seemed to be none of the honourable minister's concern.

The next morning, as I emerged from the BMC (Brihanmumbai Municipal Corporation) office at CST station and entered the subway, some bar dancers spotted me and called out to me. They were agitating against the home minister's decision at the Azad Maidan, opposite CST. They thought I was there to participate in their *morcha*, though, actually, I had no idea about it. I immediately joined their protests. I was a bar dancer myself and knew the graph of every bar dancer's life. Their only means of sustenance was now cruelly being snatched away from them, and that too by a minister who was a man and a patriarch. I decided to back the bar dancers one hundred per cent.

I participated in a TV show known as *The Big Fight*. Here I brazenly declared that Mr R.R. Patil had replaced the stage in the dance bars with a bed. Everyone knew what I meant and the statement became controversial. But I couldn't care less. The bar dancers and bar owners appealed against the state government's decision to close down the bars. The Mumbai High Court ruled in our favour, but the government looked for other ways to keep the ban in place.

I started having differences with the DWS hijras. They didn't like my no-nonsense approach. A time came when whenever something had to be done, they shirked their responsibility saying, 'We are hijras. We'll not do this and we'll not do that.' I was livid. I hated the idea of a ghetto or a gated community. Yet, that is exactly what the hijras seemed to want. I reasoned it out with them. 'What does it matter if you are a man, woman, or hijra when something's got to be done?' I asked. 'Why segregate yourselves from mainstream society to such an extent?'

But my approach did not wash with the hijras. Lataguru, too, was on their side. The DWS be damned, I thought to myself.

Nine

I met Atharva [Atharva Nair] at this juncture. He was a student at the Tata Institute of Social Sciences, Chembur. My first meeting with him was inconsequential—I got introduced to him while going somewhere. Even so, I liked his ideas and the way he expressed them. I was floored by his intelligence. I thought if we could get him to join the DWS, the society would benefit from his learning. I asked Atharva, off the cuff, if he would join the DWS. And surprise of surprises, he said 'yes'.

Atharva kept his word and joined the DWS. We became good friends, but the friendship was platonic. We were on the same wavelength, the same frequency level. Thus, Atharva knew what I wanted to say even before I said it. He is so responsive to me that even a slight inflection in my voice while talking to him on the phone, conveys to him that something is wrong. He has become a part of my life.

While work at the DWS picked up again once Atharva joined us, and we embarked on many new projects, people started to gossip. They wanted to know who this new man in my life was with whom I spent my afterhours. The worst offender here was Lataguru herself. She had become a control freak. Perhaps she was jealous. But I was not going to take it. After I became an adult, even my mother didn't probe me the way Lataguru did. I completely disliked her lack of trust.

Meanwhile, I met another hijra, Kiran—more smart and professional. Like me, she lived in Thane. She became my disciple and I made her the treasurer of the DWS. Our office was in Govandi, nearly an hour's journey by train from Thane, with a changeover at Kurla. I left my parents' house in shirt and jeans—this was still the bone of contention between my folks and me—and changed into a sari at Kiran's place. We then travelled to Thane together. The stopover at Kiran's house just to get into a sari delayed me, and we often got to work late. Then there would be a showdown with the others. Such bickering put Kiran off and she stopped commuting with me.

The gossip continued. Rumour now had it that both Kiran and Atharva were manipulating me and leading me astray. There was no basis to these rumours, for I believe I am a fiercely independent human being who follows her own inclinations.

The DSW drew international attention. In 2002 or 2003, Dorothy, a German national, visited us. She was a journalist and an Indologist. She had been to India earlier and was researching the hijras of India. She wanted to film the life of the hijras and had already thought of a title for her film—*Between the Lines*. Though Dorothy would write the script of the film, she wouldn't direct it herself. It would be directed by Thomas Wartman, a well-known German director. And it would revolve around a woman photographer who immerses herself in the world of hijras. In the process, the various facets of a hijra's life are revealed in the film. The actor chosen to play the central role was Anita Khemka, a real-life photographer. She lived in Delhi, but was to be in Mumbai in three days' time to discuss the film. I arranged to meet Anita at Barista's in Shivaji Park.

The meeting did not go off very well. Anita had her own way of looking at things, and I couldn't see eye to eye with her. Though she had observed the hijras closely, she observed them as an outsider and not as a hijra herself.

That made all the difference. In retrospect, I realize that Anita wanted to exoticize—even orientalize—the hijras, but I find such exoticism and orientalism repulsive because it 'others' us.

Our differences of opinion notwithstanding, we finally readied the script of *Between the Lines*. The film was shot in two phases. Between the two phases of the shooting, my brother Shashi got married. I attended the wedding with the rest of the family, as a result of which shooting in the second phase started late.

One of my disciples, Muskaan, also has a part in *Between the Lines*. To celebrate the making of the film, Muskaan threw a party at her place, to which she also invited Anita. When Lataguru saw Anita, she was wild with rage. She ruled that a woman had no place in a gathering of hijras, even if she was hijra-friendly. Lataguru confronted Anita and ordered her to leave. I hated Lataguru for the scene she created. Besides, where would Anita, a newcomer to Mumbai, go in the dead of night? I walked out of the party, Anita in tow, and brought her to my house in Thane.

The next day was Gokul Ashtami. There was much festivity in the air. Mumbaikars celebrate the birth of Lord Krishna in a unique way, with men dangerously perched on top of each other in a human pyramid to reach the *dahi handis* that are loaded with cash. This was new to Anita, a Delhiwallah. Lord Krishna broke the ice between us, so to speak, and we became close friends.

At last, the second phase of the shooting of *Between the Lines* was over. I was the heroine of the film! A celebrity hijra. Not that performance was new to me. I had performed on the stage in dance bars. And I was featured in a TLC programme on Mumbaikars on television. So the camera did not frighten me.

Between the Lines premiered at the Lokarno Film Festival in Switzerland in 2005. The audience swooned at my performance.

But I had my detractors too. Lataguru continued to sulk. She felt I had been co-opted by the world of glamour, and she was totally opposed to this. To her way of thinking, I was a publicity-hungry sod. She also disapproved of the fact that I lived with my parents. She was possessive and orthodox, and believed that a hijra had no right to stay with her family. 'Live with us hijras and not with your birth family,' Lataguru often reprimanded me. 'Your birth family may make you do things that are forbidden to us. We are neither male nor female. Why, then, must you cling on to the male–female society?"

To concede to her, Lataguru had a point. She thought I wanted the best of both worlds, wanted to have my cake and eat it too.

But that is not how I saw it. I did not want to live in a hijra ghetto. I wanted to be Raju to my parents; Raju, their eldest son. Though my family had reservations about my becoming a hijra, they did not turn into monsters like the families of some other hijras. So I had a duty towards them. After all, we live in a duty-bound and a shame culture. If we can be hijras without shaming our families, what's the harm in that?

Lataguru was a drama queen. Her next move flummoxed me. She came to live in the same building as me in Thane, on the floor upstairs, and urged me to live with her. 'You know nothing of hijra behaviour,' she admonished me. 'Do you even keep tabs on your disciples? They do as they please and earn us a bad name. Live with me and I will initiate you into hijra culture.'

My parents were deeply pained by the thought that I would leave home again. Like a little child, I was the object of a custody battle, with my parents on one side and Lataguru on the other. My mother was as much of a strategist as Lataguru. In order to soften her, she supplied her with a tiffin-box full of food twice daily.

But Lataguru would not be bribed. The food, which also included tea and snacks, did not have its desired effect, for Lataguru still insisted that I should live with her. I had no option but to comply.

The sari became an embarrassing issue once I started living upstairs with Lataguru. I have pointed out how I wore boy's clothes at home and changed into a sari only elsewhere, say, at Kiran's or any other hijra's house. Now, at Lataguru's, I had to be in a sari at all times. The result was that my parents, who knew I wore a sari outside, but had never actually seen me in one, had to put up with my feminine attire quite against their will. I felt trapped. I felt I lived in a golden cage. The problem was compounded by the fact that Lataguru was from our native village in Uttar Pradesh. My mother knew her long before we had become hijras. Being from our village, my parents were forced to maintain a semblance of cordiality with her.

Ten

But then, all of a sudden, Lataguru went back to live in Govandi from where she had come. That, however, did not put an end to our disputes. To make matters worse, my boredom with DWS work now reached saturation point. Once again, the feelings of hopelessness and uncertainty came over me.

A silver lining to this otherwise dark cloud appeared when I was invited to a roundtable conference in Mumbai on the status of HIV and AIDS in India. It was a high-level conference, for none other than Mr Kofi Anan, the then UN Secretary-General, was to be present. And, as chairperson of the DWS, I was one of the nine Indians invited to participate in the gig, and the only hijra, representing all the hijras of India. I was so proud.

As usual, Lataguru grumbled. She did not want me to attend the conference. My visibility bothered her.

She believed that we hijras should avoid the spotlight, the glare of publicity, and live private lives. Grapes are sour, I felt like telling her—you are dissuading me from attending the conference because you yourself aren't invited.

Dr Alka Gogate of the MDACS, on the other hand, encouraged me to go to the conference, saying it was a great honour for a hijra to be invited to such a high-level meeting. She even briefed me about what to say and what to not say in front of that august audience.

The conference took place. I was okay. But whether or not I made an impressive speech, one thing was for certain—my morale got a terrific boost.

Then I had a bad patch again. My parents were out of town, and something that Lataguru sarcastically said to me (I don't remember what) upset me so much, that I unleashed my frustration on my siblings. Actually, my brother, sister, and I were very close, but here I was, giving vent to my anger by tearing my hair and yelling at them. I felt suffocated. I felt I belonged nowhere, neither to the normal world, nor to the hijra world. I packed my bags and left and made it straight to my old friend Rahul Kale's house. He's a jolly chap with a terrific sense of humour, and I've had some fun times with him in the past. But now, though I stayed at Rahul Kale's place for two days, my mood did not change. On the contrary, it worsened. I took to the bottle, drinking like a fish and getting very drunk. Even that did not help. A whole host of existential questions kept echoing in my head: Who was I? What was I? Why did I feel unloved and unwanted?

Rahul Kale, good friend that he was, called a couple of his friends and all of us drove to Daman on the Gujarat coast, where we lived in a resort by the sea. The change, Rahul felt, would do me a lot of good. But Rahul did not have an inkling about my suicidal tendencies. Seeing the open expanse of the sea in front of me, I left my room and jumped into the sea. I wanted to die. But I wasn't allowed even that privilege, for some fishermen, who were there, dived into the water and rescued me. So much like a Hindi film! Since I was not allowed to die, I took to the bottle again. Heaven knows how much I spent on drink.

Then I met Sylvester Merchant, a trustee of the Lakshya Charitable Trust that worked for AIDS patients in Gujarat. Sylvester talked, nay counselled, me out of my suicidal thoughts, pointing out that only cowards took their own lives, and that misfortunes had to be seen as opportunities. His pep talk worked and I returned from Daman in a more positive state of mind.

For the next few days I was euphoric. I was invited to my first international conference abroad—the Sixteenth World AIDS Conference to be held in Toronto, Canada, in August 2006. And I would be going to the conference as part of a prestigious UN AIDS delegation: no mean achievement for a hijra. But then my doubts recurred. How could I go abroad? Foreign travel required a passport, and could a hijra, born as a male and now a female, ever get a passport? I did not want my passport to refer to my gender as 'male'. I wanted it to refer to me as a hijra, and a hijra alone.

I was in a dilemma: to go or not to go to the conference. As always, Lataguru, once again, proved to be the spoke in the wheel. She ordered me to accompany her to the Baba Chisti dargah in Ajmer, where there was *urs* (religious festival) going on. This is a major festival for us hijras, and to date I had never missed it. We pay homage to our forefathers at the dargah and confer the title of Saray Khwaja—the ones who walk the path of Allah—on them. Before Lataguru left for Ajmer, she gave me ten thousand rupees and asked me to follow her.

But pitted against Lataguru were my sister, my friends, and Atharva, all of whom urged me not to let go this chance of a lifetime to see the world. They pointed out that if I did not accept the conference organizers' invitation this time, it was unlikely that they would ever call me anywhere again.

I was still confused. But I finally made up my mind to go to Toronto.

The decision made, I had to deal with all the hurdles that stood between me and my flight. My passport was the first of these. Atharva dragged me to the passport office in Thane. I may have been a pessimist, but he was an optimist who believed in crossing every bridge when we got to it (without worrying too much about it beforehand).

I nervously approached the passport officer, Mr Suresh Mistri, who was seated at his desk. At first he was flustered by me and my strange demands, for no hijra had, in all likelihood, ever applied for a passport before. But once he overcame his initial bewilderment, he lent me a patient ear. When he grasped all that I said, he spoke the following words. 'I have just six months left to retire. But in my entire career not once has a hijra ever come to me for a passport. Your case doesn't have a precedent. So I really don't know what to do. I will have to contact our head office in Delhi and ask them.'

I lost hope. I thought my file would now be buried in red tape. But Mr Mistri was a helpful officer. He called his Delhi office there and then, right before me, and spoke to them for a while. As the conversation went on, my heart throbbed. I was trying to gauge from Mr Mistri's gestures whether the outcome would be positive or negative. When he finally put the phone down, he said to me, 'Yes, you can get a passport. But what is the proof that you are a hijra? We would need a registered medical practitioner to certify that you have indeed had surgery that has converted you from a man to a woman.'

I had no such certificate. And I had no such surgery done because I am not castrated. As for my other certificates, I burnt them all in a fit of rage after a fierce quarrel with my parents when I first became a hijra. I regarded this as a symbolic act because I was destroying records in which I was referred to as a male. I did not want to leave any evidence behind of my being a man once.

I was in a quandary. What was I to do? Besides, time was short. Mr Mistri had referred to a ration card. But I did not have that either because we did not renew our old ration card after shifting to our new abode. I racked my brains and remembered the name of Ms Shaila Khandge who worked at the ration office. Ms Khandge, when I met her, promised me all help, but said that things could be speeded up if I got a letter from an IAS officer. I couldn't think of any IAS officer offhand, so Shailatai took me to Mr Madhukar Pandey, who was the district superintendent of police at Thane. The officer not only gave me a certificate, but also a photocopy of his identity card! Armed with these documents, I hurried back to the ration-card office. But there were still problems. In our old ration card, my sex was stated to be male. The clerk in charge suspiciously asked me that if I was a woman, why was I described as a man in the ration card. 'Good question,' I wanted to say to him.

But the man meant business. He wasn't going to help me unless his queries were satisfactorily answered. I began from scratch, leaving out nothing about myself. It was tedious, but what choice did I have? When I was finished, the clerk almost collapsed from shock and disbelief. He asked for a glass of water and abruptly passed on my file to someone at the next table, who, in turn, passed it on to *his* neighbour. I could take it no longer. I left the ration-card office in a huff.

I now had only one alternative left: the conversion certificate. Early next morning I went to the Sion Hospital to explore the possibility of obtaining such a certificate. I spoke to the first doctor I met, who happened to be Dr Hema Jayrajani. When she heard my strange tale, she agreed to put me through a medical test. This worried me because I wasn't castrated, nor had I opted for hormone therapy that would give me the physical characteristics of a woman, breasts and such like. But Dr Jayrajani was sympathetic. She scribbled out a certificate for me that said that though I was born male, and was a male biologically, my social and psychological identity was that of a woman. This expedited matters. My ration card was ready—all I had to do was to go and pick it up.

I was exhausted. I had spent my whole day running from xerox shops to *sarkari* offices to roadside tea stalls for a quick bite. But my ordeal was by no means over. I still had to go to the passport office to get my passport, without which I wouldn't be able to leave the shores of India. I reached the passport office at Thane around three-thirty in the afternoon. I plonked down on a chair and handed my file to Superintendent Prashant Mohite's assistant. He leafed through my papers, scrutinizing every document as if I was a RAW agent. Then he pronounced his verdict: the papers were okay. Hurrah, but my passport wasn't going to be issued to me for free. It cost Rs 2,500, which was the fee at the time for an urgent passport. I looked into my handbag and found that I was short of the amount by a thousand bucks. My old friend Mistri *saab* came to my aid. He magnanimously lent me a thousand rupees. I promised I would return his money at the first opportunity, but he junked the idea and said,

'Give me only your blessings.' It was the advantageous side of being a hijra.

The next day I got my passport. I was triumphant. All the heartburn that I went through, running from pillar to post, seemed worth it now. I did not go to Ajmer with Lataguru. Instead, I went to the Sahar airport to board my Air India Jumbo.

Eleven

*B*ut before I narrate my Toronto saga, I must let something else interrupt my story. It is a photo exhibition with the caption What Are You? Curated by Tejal Shah, it featured hijras who were asked what they would like to be (if not hijras). They were then dressed up accordingly. For example, Malini, a hijra, said she would like to be a mother. She was thus dressed up as Yashoda, and her child as Krishna. When it was my turn to answer, I said I would like to be Cleopatra. Cleopatra has always fascinated me. This iconic queen of Egypt, the epitome of beauty and brains, seduced no less a king than Julius Caesar. I loved the wayward life that Cleopatra led, first marrying her own kid brother, then disguising herself as a piece of luggage to escape the civil war, and then marrying Julius Caesar. After

Caesar's death, Cleopatra had a torrid affair with Mark Antony, before poisoning herself to death.

I adored Cleopatra's zest for life. She was my role model. When I told Tejal that given half a chance, I'd like to be Cleopatra herself, she dressed me up as my goddess. I would have stayed in that garb forever had it not been time for me to board my flight.

The excitement of a journey begins with the packing. But time was so short that I had to rush through my packing. The thought that I would be sitting in a plane and landing in a foreign country for the first time in my life gave me goosebumps.

I came down with my suitcases and hailed an auto-rickshaw. Dolly, our pet dog whom I haven't referred to before, got into the rickshaw with me. Her eyes looked sad. It was as if she was begging me not to leave her. I petted her and handed her over to Shashi. Dolly came to our house fourteen years ago. She was a mere puppy back then. She remained steadfast in her loyalty to us through thick and thin. And now, I was betraying her by going away. I felt awful. Dolly's sad look haunted me throughout the flight. I couldn't stop thinking of her until I reached Toronto.

When I got back from Toronto, I learnt that Dolly was dead.

The Toronto conference opened up new vistas for me. It may have been the sixteenth international AIDS conference for others, but for me it was the first. Everything about the city, the people and the conference itself, seemed strange to me, so different from how things are in India. I regretted the fact that I did not do my homework before coming to the conference. I had no idea what I was going to say. All my time was taken up by nitty-gritty, like obtaining a passport and a visa.

The conference was well-organized. There were main sessions and satellite sessions. There was an exhibition of AIDS paraphernalia from all over the world. There were poster presentations. There was a global village—a microcosm of the whole world. It was an open forum in which everyone had the right to speak. It served as a bridge between the common man and the experts who enlightened us. And there was much else. I loved what I saw.

Before my scheduled talk, which was about the 'Hijras and Their Problems' in one of the satellite sessions on India, I was asked to substitute for a speaker who did not turn up at the transgender session, held in the global village. My speech was extempore. At first, I did not know how or where to begin, but when I started speaking, ideas flowed. When I finished, there were thunderous claps. Then it was time for my main talk. Unlike the others, I did not have a written speech. I wasn't learned. I developed cold feet. I thought it was better to listen than to speak and make a fool of myself. But then I met Yasmeen, a transgender activist from Canada. She was of Indian origin, but lived in Canada as a second-generation immigrant. Yasmeen instilled confidence in me and I made my speech, once again followed by loud applause. One of the people who congratulated me was Dennis Brown, the UN AIDS chief. 'Laxmi, I am proud of you,' he said to me. A Q–A session followed, and I was asked scores of questions about the hijra community in India. I answered them to the best of my ability and felt good. My confidence got a tremendous boost. I was now ready to take on the whole world.

And then, who should I bump into at the conference? The actress Sharmila Tagore. What's she doing here, I wondered.

When the conference was over, my friend Yasmeen took me on a sightseeing tour of Toronto city. We went to Church Street. This is the gay district of the city, where we met many trans-men and trans-women. I discovered that their lifestyle was poles apart from our lifestyle in India. In India, becoming a hijra is a spiritual process; here, it is clinical, involving counselling, surgery, and hormonal therapy. After that, the person concerned goes about his/her business as if nothing has happened. Of course there's society. It ostracizes anyone who doesn't fall in line. Trans-men and trans-women are often shown the door by their families. Their friends boycott them. They lose their jobs, they receive death threats. Many switch jobs deliberately, preferring the anonymity of a new job in a new city, where nobody knows them. But Yasmeen did not want me to go home with a dismal picture in my mind. She pointed out that things were changing, society was becoming more accepting. There were many trans-men and trans-women who faced absolutely no discrimination at all.

I felt rejuvenated when I returned from Toronto, both physically and mentally. My hairdresser there had given me a perm that made me look like an African-American, and this, coupled with the trendy clothes I had picked up from the malls, gave my appearance a facelift. I became a head-turner on the streets of Mumbai. Friends complimented me on my sartorial elegance. Even Lataguru, a hard nut to crack, came round. She did not hold my foreign jaunt against me any longer.

I was now *phoren*-returned. TV channels invited me for talk shows. Kanchan Adhikari, a TV anchor for the channel Mi Marathi, wanted me to be her guest on the show *Dilkhulas*. I was glad to be on the show, for I was by now quite camera-savvy. But the snag was that I had to speak in Marathi. Although I know Marathi, I am not that fluent in it to be able to participate in a TV programme. But then, I wasn't alone on the show. My friend Sandeep Malvi, a native speaker of Marathi, who was an adviser to the Maharashtra State AIDS Control Society, was to be my co-guest. That reassured me—if there were questions I did not understand, or could not answer, Sandeep could always take over from me. Besides, as this wasn't a live show, Kanchan, Sandeep, and I would rehearse all that we would say before the cameras were switched on.

I arrived at the studio in a one-piece suit I had picked up at Toronto. I met Sandeep in the studio and greeted him with a 'hi'. Instead of returning my greeting, Sandeep stared at me, open-mouthed. I was flabbergasted. Was something the matter? Then Sandeep spoke. 'What have you worn?' he asked me, still dazed. I guessed it. My clothes were going to have that kind of effect on everybody. I protested. 'What does it matter if I wear these clothes?' I asked Sandeep. 'After all, my body isn't exposed.' I lapsed into a little lecture about the need to destroy stereotypes. Just because I was a social worker, I didn't have to wear a sari. Sandeep relented, though

I could tell from the expression on his face that he wasn't convinced. The topic ended and the shooting began.

My Marathi did not fail me on the show. Not once did I falter. I thought I owed my competence in Marathi to the film *Pinjra* that I must have seen at least 50 times!

In my post-Toronto avatar, some of the things I did earlier seemed Lilliputian to me. Take my work at the DWS. Everyone there was so petty-minded. Their horizons were so limited. Why did I have to stick it out with such parochial people? A quarrel served as the catalyst, and I resigned from the DWS.

Kiran, Atharva, and I now founded Astitva with only a few measly rupees in each of our pockets. But we had loads of confidence and much accumulated goodwill. We also had the experience and the expertise. All this atoned for our uncertainty.

Things moved. In our very first year (2006), Anil Thanekar, who was like a son to me, got us office space just below the Dadaji Kondadev Stadium in Thane. The Avert Society cleared our pilot project on 'HIV and AIDS among the Hijras' and funded us to the tune of three lakh (three hundred thousand) rupees.

But then the Avert Society, though an NGO, was not above the bureaucracy and red tape that one finds in sarkari offices. Our MoU with them remained unsigned for some reason or the other, and the funding was inordinately delayed. The three of us were pumping in our own money to keep Astitva alive. When the funds were finally released, after six months or so, they came with the demand that we submit all accounts of the money we had spent as soon as possible. I was irritated. Astitva wasn't a multinational for its accounts to be audited. And none of us were chartered accountants!

We decided to work independently and autonomously. We immersed ourselves in welfare work, aimed at empowering the hijra community and educating society. To us, the hijras were the ultimate subaltern, deprived of fundamental rights guaranteed by the constitution. We were slaves, non-persons. We had been suffering injustice for centuries.

We embarked on a hijra census in Thane to determine their exact number, their socio-economic situation, and their source of income. We had public meetings with them to make them aware of their rights. The hijras told us that they were no different from the untouchables of the past. When they went to the District Civil Hospital in Thane (or to any other hospital for that matter), no one touched them—neither the doctors, nor the nurses, nor even the ward boys and ayahs. They were pariah.

We met Dr Pramod Chapalgaonkar, the civil surgeon of the hospital. He said, 'Henceforth, no hijra here will have any cause for complaint.' But could we believe him?

We also met counsellors and reminded them that hijras were human beings, as much in need of counselling (perhaps more), as others.

Our intervention bore fruit. A group of hijras were squabbling about something, and one of them was stabbed in the stomach. The doctors at the District Civil Hospital *first* rushed her to the operation theatre to stitch up her wounds, and only *then* did the paperwork. In Indian hospitals, patients often die as they wait to be treated, while their case papers are leisurely written out.

But how much could Astitva do? A hijra was raped in Virar. Not only did the police refuse to lodge an FIR, they refused to even listen to what the hijra had to say. The hijra was in pain. But the doctors were unwilling to treat her till the police did their job. It was a vicious circle. When I reached the police station, the havildars were in splits. They couldn't fathom how a hijra could be raped (couldn't they)? They were using the incident to lubricate their filthiest fantasies, when all they should have done was file the FIR and send the hijra to hospital.

I lost my head. Abused everyone around me—cops, doctors, I didn't care who. I called them sister-fuckers and mother-fuckers. I forced the police to file an FIR. Then I waved down an auto-rickshaw and took the hijra to the Bhagwati Hospital in Borivli. I saw that she was from the lowest strata of society.

The doctors at the Bhagwati Hospital were more civilized. The sight of a hijra did not disgust them. They assured me that the patient was out of danger, and that they would do all that was needed to restore her health.

When I came home, I buried my face in my hands and sobbed.

Twelve

May 2007. The Netherlands Transgender Film Festival was to be held in Amsterdam. *Between the Lines* would be screened at the festival. Anita Khemka was invited, but she told the organizers that she would like me to accompany her, for, after all, I was the hijra who had played the lead role in the film. 'She even has a passport,' Anita informed them, as if that was the only thing that stood between me and the festival. The real issue was funds. But the organizers of the film festival, Kamwoi and Justice Isfeld, were generous. 'You bring her along,' they said to Anita. 'We do not have enough funds, but we'll somehow manage.' Anita later told me that Kamwoi and Justice Isfeld were very happy that I was attending the festival. 'It's more than we could have expected,' they said to her. I wondered why that was so—was it because I was exotic? An Indian hijra must be quite a novelty to the Europeans.

I fell in love with Amsterdam as soon as I got there. It is truly a fairy-tale city. What streets, what hotels, what people, what climate! And everyone was so non-judgemental, unlike us. It did not matter whether one was straight or gay, man or woman, hijra or non-hijra. There was a tolerance towards all. And not just tolerance, but acceptance. It would take us more than a century to become like that.

Between the Lines intrigued the audience in Amsterdam. As in Toronto, they asked me a battery of questions here. Afterwards, I gave them a talk on the hijras of India. They found the idea of hijra gharanas and hijra *parivars* fascinating. Present in the audience was Kate Borsten, a Jewish-American transgender writer. She was born a male in 1955. As she grew up, she felt she was not a man. But if she was not a man, she had only one option: to become a woman. But then, she was sexually attracted to women as well. In the end, she opted for sex reassignment surgery and settled down in a lesbian commune in San Francisco, where she lives with her partner Barbara Karelas. But Kate's troubles were by no means over. The surgery done, she now began to feel she wasn't a woman either. Theatre provided her a way to get out of the rigmarole, and she immersed herself in it, writing and directing plays. She also wrote theoretical books on gender and sexuality. Then, she became a sort of agony aunt to teenagers who attempted suicide. She gave them pep talks to change their outlook on life. When Kate and Barbara pronounced me their daughter, I was moved. Why did so much good fortune come my way, when my fellow-hijras in India lived slavish, degrading lives?

Next, I met Stephen Whittle, born, like Kate, in 1955, as a girl child. Stephen was sickly. She had rickets from early childhood. At the age of eleven, Stephen's mother perceived that she was different from other girls. She was precocious. She spent most of her day in the library, reading tomes. She felt sexually attracted to both men and women. One of her fetishes was to become a man with a long beard and a hairy chest. At the age of twenty, Stephen actually became a man. He founded the Manchester Transsexual Group that became instrumental in changing gender laws that so far did not recognize transsexuals. In 2004, Stephen married Sara Rutherford. Through artificial insemination they had four children. They were a happy family.

I hobnobbed with other intellectuals in Amsterdam, such as Josephine Hu of Taiwan University and Susan Oxnor, an artist and owner of Amsterdam's Hotel Lloyd.

It was a rich world out there and I felt privileged to be a part of it.

Then I met Kris and fell head over heels in love with him. It was reciprocal—Kris fell head over heels in love with me, too. The *pehli nazar* was all it took, and both of us knew we were hooked. We were on our way to a party with the others, and in the car we intertwined fingers. When we got off the car, Kris asked me to proceed to the hotel where the party was to be hosted, while he slipped into an ATM booth to withdraw money. 'No,' I protested. 'I want to go with you.'

'Okay,' said Kris.

The cash withdrawn, we did not straightaway go to the party. Instead, we stood by a canal and gazed into each other's eyes. A light drizzle had just fallen. I was wearing a red *ghaghra-choli* with a silk dupatta to match. Numbed by the cold, I began to shiver. My teeth chattered. Kris saw this. He took off his shirt and threw it around my shoulders. My heart throbbed. I was intoxicated.

'Thanks, but what about you?' I asked Kris. He smiled. Then he drew me close to himself. We were about to kiss, when Kris said, 'But Laxmi, do you know who I am?'

The question jolted me out of my reverie. Just then, I saw the T on Kris's chest, which indicated that the breasts had been surgically removed. I was repulsed. So

Kris was a woman who had become a man, just as I was a man who had become a woman. The thought that I was about to make love to a woman made me shudder.

Kris mollified me. 'Give it some time,' he gently said. But I was furious. I felt betrayed by Kris's lie. I had another three or four days to while away in Amsterdam, before I returned to India. I decided not to see Kris again.

But Kris wouldn't let me be. On the day I was leaving for India, he came to the airport to see me off. I hugged him and began sobbing like a small child.

Kris stood by me as I checked in my luggage and obtained my boarding pass. I had excess luggage for which I had to pay, but did not have the money. So I gave Kris some of the stuff to keep at his house. In my heart of hearts, I thought of this as my *amanat*, which I was leaving with him. And if my amanat was with him, I was sure to return to collect it.

The plane took off. Throughout the flight, I felt as if I had left a piece of my heart behind.

I was back in Mumbai. Kris began calling me every day. The man was really in love! When the calls did not soothe his wounded heart, he went a step further—he sat in a plane and landed in Mumbai. I was in Ajmer then, but as soon as I heard that he'd arrived, I took the first available train and got to Mumbai.

I was as much in love with Kris as he was with me. But I decided to be prima donna. I cold-shouldered Kris. I did not allow his charms to mesmerize me. I was my own person and would do as I pleased. Though Kris and I slept in the same room at night, I did not let him touch me. Kris felt snubbed. He woke up at the dead of night; collected his bags, and left.

The next morning, I felt wretched. Friends like Deepak and Pravin yelled at me for treating Kris so shabbily. 'Haven't you heard of the phrase *atithi devo bhavah*?' they asked me. 'The guy travelled all the way here just to see you, but you behaved so shittily.'

When I went to Amsterdam again, I met Kris and made up with him. I apologized to him for insulting him when he came to Mumbai. Kris's friends told me that he was difficult to deal with.

❧

I took the city of Amsterdam by storm, not just as a hijra, but also as a dancer. I conducted dance workshops there that were very popular with the city's young. Indian dance is exotic to the Europeans, just as European dance is exotic to us. Susan Oxnor, whom I'd met before, curated the Amsterdam India Festival. She was bored with the usual suspects who were invited—

Hariprasad Chaurasia, Pandit Shiv Kumar Sharma, Zakir Hussain—and wanted to do something new. She took me to the festival director who said to me, 'For us, India means Laxmi.' I was flattered. It was decided that I would participate in the festival with my troupe of dancers.

When I returned to India, I had a brainwave. I called up Susan and asked her if I could bring along a troupe of hijras to Amsterdam for the festival.

'Brilliant idea,' Susan replied. 'Go right ahead.'

I got working. There were six months left for the festival, which was in November. I shortlisted the hijras who would be going with me—Simran, Manasi, Padmini, Yana. Four musicians, a male and a female singer, and a male dancer would also be part of our troupe. I had a blueprint of what we would perform at Amsterdam. But practice was the key—we would have to spend long hours rehearsing for the show. We started rehearsing at the Gadkari Rangayatan in Thane, where we could carry on uninterrupted without interference from the everyday world. Often we rehearsed until the wee hours of the morning, foregoing our meals.

Then there was this business of preparing the hijras for a foreign trip. None of them had ever been abroad before. They had to get their passports and visas, just as I had got mine. Here, my experience with the babus at the passport office obviously came handy. The hijras went through the same steps as I did, and managed to get their passports and visas with relative ease. I briefed them about the security procedures at airports, joking about how they would be frisked.

Preparation also included psychological preparation, as Western culture is so different from Indian culture. I had to ready the hijras for the mild European weather, the bland European diet, and even the sanitary habits of the Europeans. Etiquette, that bourgeois attribute, isn't a part of the vocabulary of an average hijra, but now it had to be learnt. I thought of myself as the ambassador of my country—if anything went wrong in the Netherlands before, during, or after our show, I would be putting my country to shame.

I had to shop for the show. We were going to the Amsterdam India Festival. I wanted to create an illusion of India at the venue. I wanted an ambience that was both chic and ethnic. So I bought garlands, saris, dupattas, henna, coloured powder, and dozens of miniature Ganpatis to give away as gifts—I knew from experience that westerners were greatly amused by our elephant god.

At last, the day of our departure dawned. But we did not fly together. I went ahead, while the hijras followed me a day or two later. I was thus able to receive them at the Amsterdam airport and absorb some of their cultural shock. The hijras were in high spirits the moment they were out of the airport terminal. It was early morning. Some of them pinched themselves to see if this was for real, or they were dreaming. But, no, it wasn't a dream: five hijras from India had actually set foot on European soil. They had made history.

The festival opened. Everything was picture-perfect. We presented dances from every corner of India: the lavani and *jogwa* of Maharashtra; the *raas-garba* of Gujarat; Rajasthani folk dances; bharatnatyam; *mujra*; even a Bollywood dance that got the maximum claps. We also choreographed a dance item to the pop song 'I am waiting, my lover is to come'.

The range of dances that we performed made the audience go crazy. There were catcalls and cries of 'once more'. Of course, the Amsterdam India Festival did not consist of us alone. There was a fashion show by the celebrity fashion designer Manish Arora. There was an exhibition of photographs by the Belgian photographer Mark, who had done a lot of work on the hijras of India. And there was an in-house astrologer who predicted people's futures and told them their fortunes.

So much so that BBC television made a documentary on the festival.

A month passed in a jiffy. Before we knew it, it was the last day of the festival and we were to have our closing show. There were tears in my eyes. But these were tears of both joy and sorrow—sorrow because the festival had come to an end; joy because I did something for my community.

I was fatigued and homesick. I wanted to get back home. News came that my brother Shashi had a son. His name was Anshuman. On reaching Mumbai, I went straight from the airport to see him. He was so tiny. I blessed him. He stared at me.

I kept going back to Amsterdam on some pretext or the other. One time, it was because Susan had won a prestigious award—the Beno Premsela Award of The Netherlands Foundation for Visual Arts, Design, and Architecture. Other than her family, I was the only one she invited to the function, for which she sent me a return ticket. Another time, I went to the city for a dance workshop. Even Kris attended this workshop. We still had a soft corner for each other. So when he said to me, 'Can I come to learn dance at your sessions?' I said 'yes' to him with my eyes.

Amsterdam had become my second home.

Thirteen

The standing ovation that the hijras and I got in Amsterdam for our dance performances got me anxious. Was I foregrounding my art too much and allowing my activism to take a backseat? Not that art and activism are entirely different things. They're related. In both, there is an expression of personal feelings as well as a message. Both change things, dismantle the status quo. If the world is a stage, art entertains while activism teaches. Because activism is teacherly, some people find it ponderous. They take activism to be propaganda. They think activists have an agenda. If I had to choose between the two, I would choose activism. Speaking for myself, I think I am more of an activist than an artist. And that is how I want it to be.

Perhaps I have a soft corner for activism because it saved me when I was about to perish. My visit to

Kamatipura, Mumbai's notorious red-light area, certainly played a major role in making me an activist. The sex workers of Kamatipura were unorganized and I decided to organize them. My approach was two-fold: I made the prostitutes aware of the squalor in which they lived, and I made society aware of the sordidness of the prostitutes' lives. My travels abroad aided me in my task. For example, in Toronto, I participated in a protest march of sex workers and it turned out to be an eye-opener. It gave me invaluable insights into the lives of prostitutes. I am not being condescending here, for as a hijra I could have been a prostitute too. I saw that there were women who were prostitutes by choice, and those who were prostitutes by compulsion. I began to de-link sex from morality. The prostitutes sold their bodies just as other people sold other things. Why did we make a hullaballoo about it? They were citizens of the land like anyone else, and they had the same fundamental rights as others. Why, then, didn't civil society accept them and confer respectability on them? Also, irony of ironies, their clients weren't outlaws: they were members of civil society itself.

I said these things wherever I went, and people heard me out. I was invited to be a member of bodies like the Asia-Pacific Network for Sex Workers. I was made a part of their civil society task force and sent abroad as a representative. This task force was the brainchild of no less a figure than the president of the United Nations General Assembly himself. Sex work everywhere in the world was subsumed by the AIDS endemic, and this set the alarm bells ringing. Even as I worked, I learnt.

I was going from strength to strength. One day, I got an email from UNGASS. It stood for United Nations General Assembly Special Session. I did not understand it as it was in highfalutin English. So I couldn't reply to it. Then Anita Khemka walked in and I showed her the email. She said to me, 'I hope you're going.'

'Going where?' I exclaimed.

'To New York City. For a high-level meeting of the civil society task force. All your expenses will be taken care of.'

Before I could react, Anita answered the email on my behalf. 'Yes, I'll be there,' she wrote.

I was thrilled. But my joy didn't last for long. I was worried about getting a US visa which, I was told, was a long-drawn-out and cumbersome process.

A couple of days later, I received an application form for a G4 visa. When I filled out the form and went to the American embassy, there was a mile-long queue. I stood in that serpentine queue till someone pointed out to me that for a G4 visa, I could make my way straight to the counter. I submitted my form at the counter and was interviewed by the visa officer, a surly American with a Yankee accent. As soon as the interview was over, I took a train and went to the Haji Malang shrine for a religious festival.

But my mind wasn't at ease. I was doubtful whether I, a mere hijra, would get the visa, when so many accomplished young men and women are refused visas to enter the land of plenty. The Netherlands was a different story. It was a small, non-English speaking country and not many Indians went there, except those in the diamonds business. But America was first on everyone's priority list.

The next day I got a call from the consulate. 'Your visa has arrived,' they told me. I couldn't believe my ears. An American visa in one day! It was unheard of. Then I realized that it was my G4 application that did the trick. But what was this G4 anyway?

I returned from Haji Malang, packed quickly, and headed for the airport to board my American Airlines flight. It was a long and tedious flight, as long as some of our train journeys in India. Plus, I was jetlagged. When we finally landed, there were mammoth queues at the immigration counters at JFK airport. Terrified at the prospect of joining those queues, I sat in a corner and applied lipstick. Suddenly, I heard someone call out my name. 'Laxminarayan Tripathi?' said the lady. 'You have a G4 visa? Come with me.'

I followed the kind woman and was taken to a special queue where there were just a couple of persons. In no time, my passport was stamped and I was out of the airport, while others still sweated it out in those impossible queues. That, I said to myself, pleased, is the magic of a G4 visa. But I was still intrigued by the term 'G4'. I came to the conclusion that the G stood for gay. So I had been given a gay visa—a sort of asylum visa.

I was driven to my hotel. At the reception, I gathered that our special task force comprised eleven members, some of whom were yet to arrive. I met one of them, Kiran Delli, in the lobby. When I told her that I had a G4 visa which was a gay visa, she burst out laughing. 'A G4 visa has nothing to do with being gay,' Kiran was telling me. 'It is a diplomatic visa that gives you diplomatic status. That is why you were given preferential treatment at the airport.'

I was ashamed that I had dropped a brick.

At the same time, I was on cloud nine. A hijra from India had been accorded diplomatic status in the world's richest country! It only happened in fairy tales.

I was the only transgender in the special task force. The others, who represented constituencies like homosexual men, drug users, HIV-infected people, and youth, in general, were from countries like Jamaica, Belgium, Uganda, Nigeria, Chile, and Canada.

The next day we went to the United Nations building. The flags of all the member-nations fluttered. On seeing our own tricolour, I touched it lovingly and had tears in my eyes. I was representing my beloved country at the United Nations! From where to where I had come—from the bottom of a pit to the United Nations. I was proud of myself, but with empowerment came responsibility. I was no longer just Laxmi, the hijra; I was India. I had to be careful about my etiquette and my dress, for any slip-up on my part would reflect badly on my country. Thus, the cold notwithstanding, I only dressed in saris. At meetings, I worked like a workaholic. New York has a million temptations to distract one, but I did not succumb to any of them. I didn't even join the others for a visit to Ground Zero. I just worked.

Much has been written about New York City, about its being a great melting pot, the capital of the world with Brobdingnagian energy, and so on. I can't better what has already been said, and it's best that I don't even attempt to. However, the one thing about New York that stood out for me was that here trans-men and trans-women are not obliged to live in ghettoes and gated communities, as they possibly are everywhere else in the world. Transgender people are to be found in virtually every coveted profession in New York, be it medicine, law, or IT. Contrast that with India. We abuse hijras when they 'harass' us on the streets, without realizing that the things they can do in order to survive can be counted on the fingers of one hand—begging, singing, dancing, and sex work. Can a hijra in India ever aspire to be a doctor, engineer, teacher, journalist, or business manager? The answer is a resounding NO.

Of course, it's not as if America was always the super-liberal place that it is today. While in New York, I learnt about the Stonewall Riot of 1969 that is the starting point of the LGBT movement all over the world. Several LGBT persons (as well as police personnel) lost their lives in the riot, and a memorial to honour them now stands at the site. Stonewall Inn, in New York's Greenwich Village, may truly be said to be the Mecca of the LGBT movement. America commemorates Stonewall by holding Gay Pride marches all over the country on 26 June, the day on which the riot took place.

Once again, there's a wealth of literature on Stonewall, and I cannot add to all that has already been said by people much more learned than me.

I cried when I visited Stonewall. It is Stonewall that is responsible for making America the gay utopia that it is, while the rest of the world is dystopia.

Fourteen

After New York, my civil society task force work took me to Bangkok, in Thailand. Bangkok is often regarded as the sex capital of the world and it was imperative for us to go there. While flying to Bangkok, I developed a throat infection on the plane. I also had fever. We were to stay at the Windsor Castle Hotel, and I somehow managed to reach the hotel. But I stayed in bed all day. Then Mi Gho, a co-worker who was also at the same hotel, took me to a doctor. He gave me medicine and I felt better.

On the penultimate day of my stay in Bangkok, I called up my *massi*, my mother's sister, who lives in the city. My mother and she had not met for forty years! She was stunned to hear that I was in Bangkok, and insisted that I should visit her. Her son Naren (my first cousin) would pick me up from the hotel.

Immediately, I changed from sari to shirt and jeans and scrubbed the make-up off my face. My massi and her family knew me as Raju, their nephew. They had no idea I had become a hijra.

Naren arrived in his car as decided, and before long I was at my massi's place. I hugged my massi, whom I was meeting for the first time in my life. There were tears in my eyes—I cry easily. My massi too began to weep. I called my mother in Mumbai from their landline phone and handed over the phone to my massi. The two sisters were speechless—instead of talking to each other, they just kept weeping.

The whole family gathered around me. Naren was married. His wife's name was Anjani, and they had an infant son, Ram. Then there was Shyam, Naren's elder brother. We chatted and gossiped, as we tried to catch up with the years.

Though I was dressed in boy's clothes, massi's family seemed to know about me. News of this kind has a way of spreading. But they weren't overly inquisitive. Bangkok is full of transgressive people, so a hijra is hardly a novelty. Thailand's lady boys are the equivalent of us hijras.

Just before leaving for the airport, we took a family photo to mark our reunion. Then Naren dropped me at the airport. He stayed with me as I checked my bags—one can do this in airports all over the world, except India. There was still time for me to go through security, so Naren and I chatted. When the security announcement came on a few minutes later, Naren hugged me and said, 'Bye, sister.' I was surprised. My suspicions were confirmed—my massi's family knew I was a hijra. I had gone through the charade of changing into boy's clothes for nothing. My respect for them trebled.

I was in Bangkok for just a short time, so I couldn't see much of the city, and especially its legendary nightlife. But my visit had served as a catalyst to reunite my mother and her sister. So much like a Manmohan Desai film!

Here I'd like to dwell a little on Thailand's *kathoys* or lady boys. They are a part of Thailand's famed sex industry that has patrons from all over the world, including the West, and is so 'perverse' that even an unconventional person like me was shocked. The kathoys are transgenders who cross-dress from childhood and have the body language and mannerisms of women. Some people think of them as *different* type of men, others as *different* type of women. Still others call them the 'third gender', a term that the *Kamasutra* frequently uses. The key word, of course, is *difference*. In the Thai language, the word kathoy means fairy, or queen, and the kathoys are accepted as such. Kathoys can be seen all over Bangkok as well as other parts of the country. They go to school and college, and work in shops, restaurants, beauty parlours, and even factories. And then, a large number of them are employed by the sex industry that is an offshoot, in a way, of Thailand's tourism industry. The Thais love their kathoys and treat them without bias or prejudice. Why, they even hold beauty contests for them, which are similar to those held for girls. The kathoys have the option to dress in male or female attire. Many of them go for hormone replacement therapy, breast implants, and genital reassignment surgery.

Of course, Thailand's patriarchal society, which is a lot like India's male-dominated society, first tries to dissuade a boy who wants to become a kathoy. His family, in particular, would do its best to make him change his mind. One of the reasons for this is that although kathoys have social acceptance, they're not recognized legally. Thai law does not allow people to change their gender. If they do so, they become *persona non grata*. In official documents, a kathoy would be referred to as a male. This sometimes leads to discrimination against them at the workplace. But the kathoys are not the ones to take this lying down. They have organized themselves and have their own support groups that are fighting for their rights. One of their demands is that they must be granted 'third-sex' status in passports and other government documents.

While I was in Bangkok, I met Andrew Hunter who works with Thailand's kathoys and has started the NGO Scarlet Alliance to press for their rights. I also met Kartini Slama of Malaysia, one of the country's first transgender persons to have come out. Kartini was born as a Muslim boy in an average household. By day he was the dutiful son of his parents, but by night he was a male sex worker who solicited on the streets of Kuala Lumpur. Malaysian law, like Indian law, criminalizes homosexuality, so it wasn't easy for Kartini. Sex-change operations aren't permitted. Kartini tried hard to get a job, but was always rejected on account of his sexuality. He was flustered. He was out of sync with his gender. Finally, Kartini proclaimed that he was a transgender and took to full-time sex work. Malaysia, being a Muslim country, follows the Islamic diktat that one cannot change one's god-given gender. Hence, sex reassignment surgery is prohibited in Malaysia. The ban, however, is restricted to Muslims. Thus, the majority of Kuala Lumpur's male and female sex workers are Muslims.

Kartini is religious. His religion may be intolerant towards him, but he cannot spurn it. Like him, most of his country's other sex workers, too, are religious. Since

Islam doesn't stand by them, they turn to the law for succour, hoping that the law at least will spring to their defence. But even that remains a pipe dream.

When Kartini asked me to join his Asia Pacific Network of Sex Workers as a founder-member, I readily agreed. The organization fights the exploitation of sex workers in Malaysia, Thailand, Singapore, India, Pakistan, Bangladesh, and Nepal. The efforts of the group have led to the establishment of 'transgender' as a separate identity category, whereas earlier it did not have autonomy, but was part of the MSM (Men who have Sex with Men) faction.

Activism runs through my blood. It is the elixir of my life.

Fifteen

There is the ghetto and there's the mainstream. My dominant identity was that of a hijra. I wanted to live with the hijras, but I also wanted to live in society. Luckily, for me, I was both a dancer and an activist. So, while activism enabled me to live in the ghetto, my dancing ensured that I was also a part of mainstream society.

The mass media was the route I took to be a part of the mainstream. As I have already said, my first TV appearance was on the show *Boogie Woogie*, where I was merely a member of the audience. Next, small films came my way, some of which remained in the cans and never got released. I was in a Punjabi music album titled *Na Re Baba Na* choreographed by Joe Khan. I had bit roles in soaps like *X Zone* and films like *Aashiq*, and then, of course, my big break came in Vaishali Samant's *Lavani* on *Fire* and Thomas Wartman's *Between the Lines*. Why, I was even on international TV channels—TLC did a documentary on Mumbai titled *Six Degree Planet* and, sure enough, I was in it!

When Mumbai's bar dancers filed a case against the arbitrary closure of the bars by the High Court, I found myself going to court often. One day, I met Smruti and Nishta Jain at the court. They were interested in the case in their capacity as film-makers and activists and attended hearings often. We got introduced, and after some small talk, Nishta asked me to see her the next day. But the next day I wasn't in my element. Something bothered me, and I don't recall what it was. Still, I went to see Nishta. To cheer me up, she took me out for a walk and we talked about this and that—about food, about exercise, and about sexuality. Nishta had been invited to make a short film for the Kala Ghoda Festival held in Mumbai in February each year. But she did not have a subject. Suddenly, Nishta turned to me and said, 'Laxmi, why don't I make a film about you?' And that was that— the film got made. It is the story of a highly strung but rebellious hijra who rips off the masks of morality worn by the middle class. Nishta wanted the film to have a provocative title, and I suggested that she call it *Slut*. 'Brilliant,' said Nishta, and that was the title that came to stay.

There are hijras galore in India, but somehow I was the chosen one, chosen to be the public face of the hijra community in media. After *Slut*, I appeared in the documentary *Bambaiya*, made by Kartikeya Narayan Singh. The film explores Mumbai's relationship to sex from different angles—from sexual traditions to people's sexual preferences. The film's pivotal characters include a filmmaker, a hijra, and a hockey player. I play myself in the film—I am Laxmi, the hijra and the transgender activist.

It is one thing to act and dance in front of TV cameras, and quite another to participate in live discussions. In such programmes, I was handicapped by the fact that I wasn't as educated as some of the other panellists. At times, I was too upfront during such discussions and put people off. In this context, I especially remember the show *Mahacharcha*, where I aggressively bickered with a panellist while the cameras were on. This recurred in another show, *Aamne Saamne*. But in both shows, the audience disagreed with the point of view of the panellists and agreed with me. I don't know if they were patronizing me as the only hijra on the show.

My television appearances made me a known face. Strangers often accosted me on the street to ask, 'You are Laxmi? I saw you on TV and liked you.' Laxmi, the hijra, was on her way to stardom.

During my childhood.

At Talavpali, Thane.

During model-coordination days.

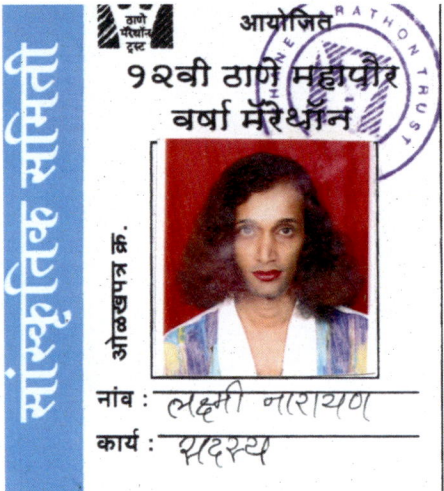

Varsha Marathon
I-card.

At Hajimalang
with sisters.

At a get-together. From L to R: Laxmi, Shabina, Unknown, Shabnam, Unknown, and Priya Babu.

At a performance at World AIDS Day for MDACS, 2002.

From the 'Dream Series', dressed as Cleopatra. Photograph courtesy of Tejal Shah.

At Amsterdam India Festival, where transgenders performed lavani for the first time.

With Kamal.

With Shahin and Muskaan.

At the Sixteenth World AIDS Conference, Toronto, Canada, 2006, where I was on the plenary representing transgender issues.

With Chaya Haji and other community members.

My father, Chandradev
Chandinath Tripathi.

My mother,
Vidyawati Tripathi.

Birthday
celebration with
Papa, Mom,
Shabhoo Bhai,
and sister's
father-in-law,
Mr Mishra.

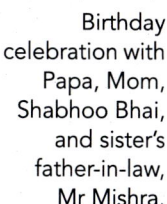

At my birthday party with my family. Photograph courtesy of Anita Khemka.

With Salman Rushdie during my interview for his article in *AIDS Sutra*.

With Salman Khan on the set of *Dus Ka Dum*.

With Atharva and Nisha at Kamatipura Lane No. 1. Photograph courtesy of Anita Khemka.

At a sex workers' rally in Delhi.

With Ashok Row Kavi and Vivek Anand. Photograph courtesy of Punit Reddy.

With Lataguru. Photograph courtesy of Punit Reddy.

With Prince
Manvendra.

With Andrew Hunter. Photograph courtesy of Marc De Clercq.

With Susan Oxnor. Photograph courtesy of Marc De Clercq.

Being me.

In moving thoughts while moving through traffic. Photograph courtesy of Anita Khemka.

In Melbourne. Photograph courtesy of Punit Reddy.

With Deepak Salvi.

With Pravin Balaya.

With Dorothy at the Koovagam Festival, Tamil Nadu. Photograph courtesy of Marc De Clercq.

Of course, I am not suggesting that the ambivalence in people's attitudes towards hijras disappeared altogether. It was still there. To many men and women, we were extraterrestrials.

Then Salman Khan called me. It was the 4th of May 2008.

Salman wanted me to participate in his TV show *Dus ka Dum*. But I was to fly to New York for an activists meet that very day. Salman persuaded me to cancel my ticket and book another one for the next day, saying he would do this for me himself. But I played hard to get. 'I'm sorry,' I told the famous film star. 'The hijras are more important to me than you.' Of course, in my heart of hearts I wanted to be on the show, for Salman was my matinee idol and I was willing to lick the dust off his feet. So what do I do? I shoot for the show all day, and catch my flight to New York that same night.

When I returned from New York, a plum assignment came my way. I participated in the TV show *Sach Ka Saamna*, adapted from the American television programme *Moment of Truth*. This programme dragged people's private lives into the public arena, and eventually got so controversial that it had to be taken off the air. The format was as follows: participants were asked intimate questions about their sexual lives in the presence of an audience, which included their own family members. The truth (or otherwise) of the answers was verified by a lie detector. In my case, my parents, my sister-in-law Sapna, Deepak, my man Friday, and my chela Shahin were with me on the show. I answered fifteen out of the twenty-one questions put to me honestly and won ten lakh rupees. Then the sixteenth question flummoxed me and I was out.

But first, let me say what some of the fifteen questions were. One of them was about whether my family had accepted me as a woman, though I was born as a boy. My answer was 'no' and it was the correct answer. To my family, I remained their eldest son. The cameras turned to my father, and he said, 'Laxminarayan is my eldest son and he will continue to be so as long as I am alive. As the eldest son, he is heir to my property in Mumbai and Uttar Pradesh, and my younger son, Shashinarayan, comes after him.'

Another question was, 'Did you avoid going out with your parents for fear that it would humiliate them?' I answered 'yes' and again it was the correct answer. I followed this up with a lengthy explanation: I was afraid that my being a hijra would embarrass my parents, and so I never accompanied them to family functions. What if someone asked them if I was their son? The poor souls would not know what to say. But I was wrong. My parents were not ashamed of me. They did not ask me to leave the house when I became a hijra. At Shashi's wedding, I was given my rightful place as the eldest son of the family. I was not even asked to cut my long hair, though I was willing to keep away from the ceremonies if my long hair was a problem.

My father chipped in, 'Why should I expel Laxmi from the family? I am his father, he is my responsibility. A hijra can be born to any family. If we spurn them and show them the door, we leave them with no alternative but to become beggars. Driving Laxmi out of the house was out of question.'

And yet another question was, 'If the last wish of your parents is that you live the life, not of a hijra, but of a man, would you comply?' I said 'no' though my parents were there, and it turned out to be the right answer. I reiterated that I would never live the life of a man.

Papa chipped in again, 'If one is a BA, LLB, and has been a practicing lawyer for fifteen years, can he suddenly become a doctor and start practicing medicine? Can he suddenly become an engineer? Likewise, if one is a hijra, one can't suddenly become a man. I have no right to interfere in my son's life.'

Papa's answer brought tears to my eyes. How many hijras in India could boast of such supportive parents? It was quite the opposite with most hijras—their families emerged as the biggest villains of the piece. I was indeed lucky.

The sixteenth question was a googly. I was asked if I had ever had sex with a woman. I took my time and mulled over the question. Before I became a hijra I was a homosexual lad. So having sex with a girl was out of question. Then I became a hijra. Hijras are not permitted to have sex with women. Even so, I was in love with Kris who was once a woman. Then there was another woman I was sexually attracted to, but my physical intimacy with her did not go beyond foreplay, though foreplay there was. I was confused. Should I say 'yes' or 'no'? My time was running out. I finally answered 'yes'.

That was the *wrong* answer. I had to quit the show. To the lie detector, mere foreplay wasn't sex.

Bigg Boss. That's the name of a popular TV show. There's no one who hasn't heard of it. And one fine morning, I get a call from the production house that produces the programme and am asked if I would like to take part in it. For some reason, they think I am an advocate and ask for 'advocate Laxmi' on the phone. Perhaps, they were mistaking 'advocate' for 'activist'. Who knows? Two of my chelas, Sara and Rachna, were with me when the call came. Both of them kept nudging me to say 'yes'. But there was a catch. The rules of the show required participants to be locked up in a house where the shoot took place for three whole months. That was a long time! Papa was unwell. How could I abandon my mother and the rest of the family for such a long time? But was I the one to jettison an opportunity to become famous? I thus signed up for *Bigg Boss*.

I now had to decide whether I would be on the show as Laxmi the person, or Laxmi the transgender activist. I opted for the latter. I wanted to use the show as a platform to make viewers aware that hijras are normal people, just like them. We're not extraterrestrial. We have emotions, just like ordinary human beings, and are perhaps more sensitive than them. It was 2 October, Gandhi Jayanti day, when I entered the *Bigg Boss* set, nay house, as a spokesperson for the hijra community.

Fourteen of us were locked up in that house. Among them were famous film stars like Pooja Bedi and Shakti Kapoor. Then there was Pooja Mishra, Mahak Chahal, Vida Samadzai, Juhi Parmar, Mandeep Bahalvi, Rageshwari, and a few others. The show was hosted by

Sanjay Dutt and my heartthrob Salman Khan, whom I had met before. 'Hi, Laxmi,' Salman was now saying to me, making everyone envious.

The first three or four days were fun. But after that, everybody showed their true colours. People were stressed, grouchy. But then, that is the whole point of the show—to create everyday situations in which people can be assessed on the basis of their reactions. The show was an eye-opener to me. I had no idea a house could emit such negative energy. We literally got on each other's nerves. And all the while the cameras were left on to capture our natural moods. It was reality television at its worst. But when the cameras were switched off, all was hunky-dory again. In my case, I was pampered by Salman Khan and Sanjay Dutt. I still recall my tête-à-tête with them. I realized I was in love, not with Salman as a person, but with his personality. He is so straightforward. The two of them, Salman and Sanjay, always referred to me as 'Laxmiji'. The suffix '*ji*' is reserved for people worthy of respect. It has never been used for hijras. And here I was, a hijra, being addressed as 'Laxmiji' by two distinguished film stars. What more could I ask for? I think, seeing me laugh, cry, eat, drink, and bicker like everyone else during the shoot, made people realize that we hijras are ordinary mortals like them. We do not exist in a rarefied realm.

Three months passed.

When I emerged from the sets of *Bigg Boss*, I was besieged by the media. I felt like Amitabh Bachchan.

Sixteen

$\mathcal{B}$ut highs are often followed by lows. Still gloating over my performance in *Bigg Boss*, I got thrown out of a Bombay Gymkhana party. The occasion was, as usual, a sexuality conference to which I had been invited as a speaker. In the evening, a dinner party was hosted for delegates at the Bombay Gym, to which I also went. Initially, I was welcomed by the society ladies at the reception, and was even hugged by them. Then, the organizers, Ajay and Parvesh, greeted me and led me to a hall upstairs where the party was in progress. Among the first guests I was introduced to at the party, were the couple Shreela and Mahesh Mathai, who owned the high-end restaurant Blue Frog, where some of the conference proceedings were held. I stealthily glanced around, liquor glass in hand, and noticed that some people recognized me and smiled. I waved and smiled back. But, somehow, I wasn't comfortable in that gathering of snobs and wanted to take my leave. The Mathais would not hear of it. They finally agreed to let me go only after I'd eaten, and, accordingly Shreela brought me a plate full of food. I munched and chatted.

All at once, the CEO of Bombay Gymkhana, Brigadier R.K. Bose, entered the party hall and called Ajay aside. Ajay's face paled. What started as hush-hush talk between Ajay and the Brigadier, now snowballed into a fierce quarrel. I knew that something was amiss. The Mathais, too, were flabbergasted.

A few minutes later, Ajay approached me with tears in his eyes. He told me I would have to leave the party, for club rules did not allow people like me to enter the Bombay Gymkhana. Ajay was appalled, but helpless all the same, for Brigadier Bose had threatened to revoke his membership if I did not make my exit at once. I was not even allowed to finish my food.

Crestfallen, I left the Bombay Gymkhana despite the protests of my friends. I couldn't believe that I was being shown the door on account of my sexuality and identity. I decided to speak to the newspapers about the incident. Vishwas of *Mumbai Mirror* agreed to expose the club on the front page of his tabloid newspaper provided

I gave him an exclusive story and did not speak to other journalists. But once the story leaked, I began getting calls from newspapers left, right, and centre.

I was so outraged that I began telling all and sundry about the way I had been humiliated. Vishwas kept his word, and the next morning I woke up to a screamer headline in the *Mirror* that blew the incident out of proportion, somewhat to my embarrassment. My mobile did not stop ringing that day, with friends from four corners of the world, so to speak, calling me to express their indignation.

I sent Bombay Gymkhana a legal notice through my friend Anand Grover of the Lawyers' Collective, who is an ardent supporter of the LGBT movement. I demanded a public apology from the club and from its CEO, Brigadier R.K. Bose. The case was admitted on grounds of discriminatory behaviour on the part of the Bombay Gymkhana. But then half-way through the case, I lost interest and decided not to fight it. I put the matter behind me.

The Bombay Gym episode motivated me to fight for transgender rights with renewed vigour. Some of us hijras filed a complaint against the Government of India, alleging that we were denied our basic rights. One of the issues we raised was that in all government application forms, one had to state one's gender as either male or female. But hijras are neither male nor female. That meant that we couldn't fill out application forms! Which, in turn, implied that a hijra couldn't get a passport or a ration card as a hijra. The clerks in the government offices were confounded. If hijras were neither M nor F, what were they? We suggested that we were O, or other, and that, henceforth, all application forms should have an option for 'O'. We made the babus in the sarkari offices see that this small step on their part would make a gigantic difference in the lives of hijras, who could then apply for government jobs, procure bank loans, and cast their vote. In any case, that is what the National Human Rights Commission had ruled.

Hijras are considered to be ugly people. I wanted to reverse that mindset. And I thought of doing it by organizing a beauty pageant for the members of my community. If there are Miss India and Miss Universe contests for women, why not for hijras, I asked myself. Hijras are called born-clappers, but, for a change, we would get the world to clap for us. The sheer sensational-ism of the idea got many event managers to approach me with packages. But I turned all of them down. If a beauty contest for hijras was to be organized, I would do it myself.

But then I realized that an outfit called Najakat had already beaten me to the idea. They organized an annual hijra beauty contest that was sponsored by a charitable group known as V-Care. I told the founder of V-Care, a man named Sunil Saldhana, who was the friend of a friend, that I, too, would like to hold a hijra beauty contest. He jumped at the idea, giving me a carte blanche as far as funds were concerned. 'Do it. We have crores,' he told me. 'Do it at an all-India level.'

I got working. A little while ago, two friends and I had started a company called Twelve Noon Entertainment. So I thought of doing the beauty contest under its auspices. We came up with a title for the event—we would call it the Indian Super Queen Contest. Ranjit and Amit, the two friends with whom I had started Twelve Noon Entertainment, liked the idea.

We decided to have auditions in ten major cities—Mumbai, Delhi, Kolkata, Chennai, Ahmedabad, Bengaluru, Hyderabad, Indore, Jaipur, and Bhubaneshwar. This would be followed by a semi-final and then final in Mumbai, the city of cities. My friend Anita Khemka was appointed as the official photographer of the contest.

For the first time, a hijra beauty pageant was being organized in India on such a large scale. Hijras, who averted the gaze of others because of a deep and abiding inferiority complex, would now be walking the ramp! Many of them were on stage for the first time in their lives. Some experienced stage fright, but others helped them overcome it.

The hijras were exhilarated. Everywhere, we were the talk of the town. The contest boosted their confidence and they were able to carry themselves about with an air of dignity.

I travelled with the unit to all ten cities. As I tend to be sickly, with asthma sapping my energies, I needed my friends and chelas to be around me to fuss over me. And they did so unfailingly. Atharva, Anita, Annu, Shahin, and Komal were there by my side at all times to keep me away from harm's way. The Indian Super Queen Contest owes its success to them in no small measure.

Then financial troubles came my way as Sunil Saldhana of V-Care went back on his word. I was at the Jaipur airport after an audition when I got a call from my office. I was told that Sunil Saldhana had phoned to say that he wouldn't be able to pay us the three to four crores he had promised. The maximum he would pay us is one-and-a-half crore, and we had to manage the contest with that amount.

I was shocked. This was a thunderbolt. I barely comprehended what my office colleague told me on the phone. I had incurred expense on the basis of the budget Saldhana had originally promised us. How was I to clear my debts now? I thought of calling off the contest altogether. I was so tense I thought my heart would stop beating. To call off the contest would be to accept defeat. And I wasn't born to accept defeat. It went against my personality to retreat from something I had wilfully started. I did not want to withdraw from the contest. Atharva agreed with me. But we decided that, for the moment, we would withhold auditions in tier-two cities like Indore and Jaipur. This would ease our financial burden to some extent. We would directly hold the semi-final and final in Mumbai, which was our base. Saldhana's one-and-a-half crore would then suffice.

The actor Seema Biswas kindly consented to be the referee for the semi-final. As for the final, we held it at the Grand Maratha Hotel, close to the Sahara International Airport. We had an illustrious panel of judges comprising Celina Jaitley (who was with us from the very start), the legendary film star Zeenat Aman, my mentor Ashok Row Kavi, Kartini, Malaysia's first transgender activist, and R.J. Malishka. Our Indian Super Queen contest was being held on a scale as grand as any Miss India or Miss Universe contest.

I received high praise for my work and was euphoric. But my joy was neutralized by my father's illness. Papa was suffering from cancer of the mouth that had been detected about six months ago. He had been operated once and was now undergoing chemotherapy. I felt guilty at not being able to sit at his bedside and attend to him, he who had been such a supportive parent to me. But then my father had others in the family to look after him, whereas the hijras had none besides me.

Calamities have a way of appearing at the same time. As if Papa's illness wasn't visitation enough, my brother Shashi now lost his job because of the economic meltdown. Wisely, he decided not to look for another job at once because he was needed at home to attend to our father, while I chased and pursued fame.

Seventeen

My father, Chandradev Chandinath Tripathi, was from a small town named Bhita, near Gorakhpur in eastern Uttar Pradesh. He was a Brahman, and, therefore, well known in the region, and well respected too. My grandfather, before my father, was also revered for his knowledge of the Vedas and the Upanishads. The Tripathis were a prosperous family. There was always a plentiful supply of food grains in the house. The numerous visitors who came to the house were never allowed to leave without a meal.

Our generation did not quite appreciate the value of our lineage. We squandered away our heritage. Truth to tell, the decline began during the time of my grandfather itself, for his brothers and he became rivals, and they frittered away all that we had. My father's generation was heir to this family feud. In the feudal set-up of rural

Uttar Pradesh, it was common for kith and kin to murder each other for a slice of the pie. My grandfather did not exactly do that, but he mercilessly beat up my father on more than one occasion, and finally chucked him out of the house, saying he was a blot on the reputation of the family. Perhaps, in his heart of hearts, he cursed my father saying he would give birth to a hijra.

As the storyline of many a Hindi film goes, when my father was thrown out of the house, he caught the first available train and headed straight for Mumbai. A relation in Mumbai got him a nondescript job that enabled him to keep body and soul together. But my father meant business. Knowing he had nowhere to go, he worked honestly and sincerely, and picked up the pieces of his life. A time came when he had saved enough to be able to send money home. He even managed to invite some of his vagabond cousins to Mumbai to set them up in this dream city.

My mother was also from Uttar Pradesh, from a town called Banhava to be exact. Her name was Vidyawati. She married my father and bore him seven children, of whom only three survived. Foremost on the priority list of my parents was the need to instil values in their children. That paid off. I believe I am what I am today on account of those values.

Mother was an early riser. She woke up at five in the morning to start the household chores. My father also rose early and left the house at six—a strange hour to leave for work. I was closer to my mother than to my father. In fact, my father and I rarely spoke. There was a barrier between my father and I that made it difficult for me to open up to him. Later, I gathered that many gay sons experience a breakdown of communication with their fathers.

My brother Shashi was different. He was a prankster from the word go. While crossing a busy thoroughfare on our way to school, he would suddenly let go of my hand and sprint across the road. If I reprimanded him, he bit my hand. When I complained to my parents, they invariably took his side, saying he was only a kid brother. I fumed at the injustice. I was a kid, too. Yet, just because I had a younger brother, I was treated like a grown-up. That's always the fate of first-borns, but it isn't fair. The result was that I grew up before my time and did not have much of a childhood.

Time passed. Shashi grew up, too, and soon it was time for his marriage. I have already stated that he got married to Sapna—it was an arranged marriage—and they had a son, Anshuman. Now, little Anshuman was the baby of the house, whom everyone mollycoddled. As for me, my relationship to Anshuman was special: I was his hijra auntie whose blessings would always bring him good luck.

Actually, I wasn't a first-born. My sister was older than me. She gave me my very first dancing lessons and moulded me as a dancer. But then she married a *fauji*, Wing Commander Jitendra Mishra, and settled down with him at virtually the other end of India, in Assam. This was before I became a hijra. Of course, an armed forces job is a transferrable job, and there were times when my *jijaji* was posted in nearby cities like Pune. But then he was also sent to Malaysia. That my sister lived in faraway places was perhaps a blessing in disguise, for my identity as a hijra was unacceptable to her soldier husband. Army men tend to be macho, and masculinity means a lot to them. As I have said earlier in my account, when I became a hijra, my folks were not concerned about anyone else as much as they were concerned about my sister. They feared the worst, thinking her husband and his parents would send her back to her *maike* for the shame she had heaped on them. And their fears were not exaggerated or farfetched—my jijaji did, in fact, stop talking to me for many years afterwards. His father, too, a rationalist and masculine to his fingertips, thought of me as an odd ball, though when my own father died, he stood by us like a pillar of strength.

Papa's diagnosis commenced with a mouth ulcer on his inner lip that refused to heal. We had it tested and it turned out to be malignant. Papa was a high-risk contender for oral cancer, for he had been a gutkha addict from the age of ten. His diagnosis set a chain reaction of tests, biopsies, surgeries, and chemotherapy. We couldn't bear to see him in so much pain. I wanted to cry, but then again, as the eldest son, I had to be brave. Boys don't cry. Though I wasn't a 'boy' in the conventional sense, I had to put up a show of masculinity that drained me. There came a stage when the doctors recommended that we take Papa off all life-support systems that, given his deteriorating condition, were pointless anyway.

The clock was ticking. To complicate matters, a spate of invitations to prestigious international events came my way. I had become so ambitious, so big for my boots, that it was impossible for me to turn any of them down. They hung over my head like the proverbial sword of Damocles. When I left for the airport, would I be seeing my beloved father for the last time? Would I return only to attend his funeral?

The first conference was in Bangkok. I sat in the front row. People spoke, but my brain registered nothing. I went to the lobby and burst out crying. Vivek Anand (of Humsafar Trust) noticed this and came up to me to console me. I hadn't had a wink of sleep. I was on the hotline to Mumbai 24X7. When I did doze off, nightmares startled me out of bed at the dead of night. I dozed off again at the airport on the way back home. When my eyes opened a few minutes later, I asked Prince Manvendra, who was seated next to me, if we had reached Mumbai! He looked at me as if I were demented. 'Be cool, sister,' he said to me.

The second conference was in Barcelona. In the evening, I strolled down the Ramblas. I wanted to buy something for Papa, as I always did during my foreign jaunts, but couldn't decide what to buy. Scary images of his wasted face contorted with pain flashed before my eyes. What use did he have of my gifts? I wish I could find a magic potion on the streets of the city that would save his life. I returned to my hotel and burst into tears.

The stress took its toll on me. I fell ill in a strange land and had to be rushed to hospital in an ambulance. I had spells of dizziness and breathlessness and wondered if I was going to die. But I kept my family in the dark about my condition, for they already had my father's illness to contend with. I stayed in the hospital for five days. Then I returned to Mumbai.

Papa's condition had worsened. But that did not stop me from going to my third conference, this time in Vienna, Austria. I had become a globetrotter. I rationalized the situation. I was invited to inaugurate the conference's 'global village'. Where on earth was a hijra given such honour? I owed it to my community to go to the conference and do them proud. At the same time, I was concerned about my father. I went to the conference, my heart still in Mumbai, and returned as soon as it was over. I did not join the others on sightseeing trips in and around Vienna, one of Europe's most beautiful cities.

My father's health fluctuated. At times he was better, at times at death's door. Our sleep patterns grew erratic as we kept a constant vigil. There were nights when we did not sleep at all. On other nights, it was almost dawn, the cock-crowing hour, before we managed to catch some sleep. The thought that fate might snatch Papa away from us was unbearable.

It was the night of Saturday, 7 August. I was out in the city when my mother frantically called me and asked me to get home as soon as possible. My father was sinking. Even his morphine injections were doing him no good. Mom's call set the alarm bells ringing in my head. Had my father's time come? When I reached home, I found the whole family and some of my chelas seated around Papa. He groaned in agony. But then, almost miraculously, his pain subsided and he felt better. To relax me, my chelas took me to a bar where we sat drinking till three in the morning. After that, I went back home to find my sister and her daughter sprawled on my bed. Sleep eluded them even at that unearthly, godforsaken hour. I played with my niece.

The next day, Sunday, was the last day of the month of Ashadh. It was the day the people of Maharashtra refer to as '*guttari*'. That's because they drink so much that they fall into gutters and lie there all night. After that, all drinking (and eating of meat) is banned for a whole month. My mother screamed out to me as I was about to go to her room with a hot cup of tea. I rushed downstairs to find Papa moaning in a half-dead way, and Mother rubbing his chest to revive him. Shashi was also there, fiddling with the numerous tubes attached to Papa's body. I panicked and called the doctor, asking if we could bring the patient to him.

'Laxmi,' the doctor was telling me, 'if you want my advice, I'd say let the old man die in peace. Don't add to his torture by pumping him with more medicines and injections because they're not going to help. The final decision, of course, is yours and the family's.'

I sat by Papa's pillow. The doctor's words made sense. Whatever it was, I wanted my beloved father's suffering to come to an end. There was a blank look in Papa's eyes.

It was as if he was saying to me, 'Raju, I'm going. Now, as the eldest son, you've got to take care of the family.' I took Papa's hands in mine. He closed his eyes.

Deepak came. He gave Papa a look and took me aside. 'Laxmi, Papa has passed away,' he said. I did not know how to break the news to the family. I paced the room, my heart beating fast.

Subsequently, Dr Mishra arrived and confirmed that Papa was dead. I grew numb with grief.

Eighteen

News of Papa's death spread quickly, and in no time relatives and friends converged in the house. I cannot think of any close or distant relative who wasn't there. I felt orphaned. What would we do without Papa? My mother beat her breasts and wailed. She had become a widow.

The rituals of our caste have it that the one who lights the dead man's funeral pyre must stay in seclusion for eleven whole days. I couldn't afford to absent myself for that long, as there were a whole lot of formalities associated with Papa's death that had to be dealt with. Hence, it was decided that Shashi would light the funeral pyre, while I stayed free to attend to the nitty-gritty. Some may say it was just as well that a son, and not a hijra, lit the funeral pyre of his father. In my heart of hearts I was sad. I couldn't spend time with Papa when he was alive. And now, I was being denied the chance to consign his body to the flames.

Papa was cremated. Among us Brahmans, death rites can be as elaborate and as expensive as wedding rites. Three priests preside over the obsequies. There is an extended period of mourning, during which the bereaved family eats non-spicy sattvic food, devoid of even turmeric and salt. The one who lights the funeral pyre cooks and eats separately. At the end of ten days, the clothes of the deceased and of his bereaved family members are disposed of, and a barber shaves their heads. Then, on the eleventh day, there's a feast, known as *narayan bali*. First the Brahmans are fed, and then the others eat. The women of the house are the last to be served. The Brahmans are also given gifts, known as *daan*. They can ask for anything—land, houses, gold— and it has to be given to them, or else the dead man's soul will not rest in peace. Such blackmail!

Naturally, all this requires pots of money. There were travelling expenses, too, for the rituals had to be conducted in Papa's native place, far away from Mumbai. And while he was alive, Papa's medical bills ran into thousands, if not lakhs, as he had no medical insurance. The money I earned from TV shows like *Bigg Boss* and *Sach ka Saamna* was stashed away in fixed deposits and could not be cashed. We were thus left with no option but to borrow. The onus fell on me, and scarcely twenty-four hours after Papa's death, I found myself decking up to go out and look for money. Tears streamed down my cheeks and smudged the make-up I had worn.

Call it sympathy, call it goodwill, but people did not cringe when lending me money. They lent it wholeheartedly. We bought tickets and started for our hometown. We travelled by train, not just because it is cheaper than plane, but also because we wanted to use the two-day journey to calm our nerves a little, especially my mother's.

The train pulled into Gorakhpur station early morning. Some relatives received us at the station. Soon we were off to my hometown. On reaching my hometown, I noticed a large number of white ambassador cars with red beacon lights on their roofs parked near our ancestral home. Imagine how puzzled I was to learn that ministers came in these cars to meet me! The whole town gaped in amazement as one *mantri* after another came up to me to offer his condolences.

Some cousins of mine lived in the town. They were sons of my father's eldest brother, who was now dead. His wife, when she was alive, took *panga* with my parents all the time, though she was nice to us, the children.

My father's eldest brother—my *chacha*—had three sons. Their names were Rammohan, Shyammohan, and Krishnamohan. He also had two daughters, Bindu and Urmila. Since Rammohan was dead, Shyammohan was considered to be the eldest son of our extended family by all of us. We addressed him as '*Bade Bhaiya*'. My father did not differentiate between his own sons and those of his brother. He considered Shyammohan to be his oldest son. However, during Papa's illness, Shyammohan never once came to Mumbai to see him. This wasn't done, and now the entire clan that had assembled there thought that we would have it out with my cousin, and there would be a showdown.

I anticipated this, and accordingly, briefed my mother and brother on the train about what to say, and what not to, once we reached our hometown. Still, petty-minded neighbours tried to instigate a quarrel by asking us, in Shyammohan's presence, what ailed him, and whether he would be willing to give us our share of the land. We remained unprovoked. I snubbed some of the gossipmongers in that crowd by asking them to mind their own business.

We carried Papa's ashes with us to our hometown. One of Papa's last wishes was that he should die in his native place. Since that was not to be, mother defied custom, and carried his ashes with her to the house. She tied the earthenware pot containing the ashes to a window, and said to anyone who looked askance, that she was merely fulfilling her husband's wish—if he couldn't come there in person, let his mortal remains at least sit there for a while before they were immersed in the holy Ganga.

The next day, we left for Varanasi to immerse the ashes in the Ganga. Shahin and Shyammohan accompanied me. On the way, Shyambhaiya expressed regret at not being able to be with Papa before his death. He started to cry. I urged him to let bygones be bygones, and, on impulse, handed over the urn containing Papa's ashes to him to cast into the river. Again, I heard voices in my head saying it was just as well that a brother's son, and not a hijra, was immersing my father's ashes into the water. We stepped into the boat and the boatmen rowed us midstream. It was sunset. I joined my hands in a prayerful gesture towards the setting sun. The sun was setting now, but would rise again tomorrow. But Papa was gone forever and would never return. Shyambhaiya spilt the ashes into the river. As the river swallowed the ashes, I burst into tears—the last remnants of my father's memory were snatched away from me.

When I got back, a crucial issue stared me in the face: I had to tonsure my head. According to custom, at least one man in the family had to tonsure his head on the tenth day of a person's death, when the *sutak* or period of 'pollution' ends. Though I was a hijra, Papa always regarded me as a son, a man, and as his eldest son, it fell upon me to give up my hair. This, however, I did not have the heart to do. How could a hijra go about with a shaved head? But none saw merit in my argument. They told me the story of a man who refused to shave off his moustache when his father died. The result? Whenever he tried to perform the last rites of his father, something came in the way, and he wasn't able to perform the rites. Then he shaved off his moustache and all was well—the rites were performed and the father's soul was liberated.

But then I had a brainwave. I had read somewhere that yogis, *yakshas*, *kinnars*, and *gandharvas* did not have to shave off their hair when their kin died. I told the elders who had gathered there that I was a kinnar, and that did the trick. My erudition impressed them, and I got away with shaving off just a single lock of my hair as a symbolic gesture.

On the eleventh day, the narayan bali marked the end of the period of pollution. Three Brahmans arrived at our place in the morning. I was well versed with all the rites and rituals, so it was impossible for them to fool me. My uncle Gopalchacha remarked, 'Raju knows all the rites and rituals. No one can hoodwink us.' The Brahmans took Gopalchahcha's word for it, and the ceremonies, which they hurriedly complete in an hour or two, went on till evening. Then the food was prepared. Around a thousand people came to partake in this *barakhana* or feast. That spoke of Papa's popularity—of the love and respect that the people of our town had for him.

Just before the food was served, there was the distribution of gifts. As I have said, the Brahmans who preside have the right to ask for anything, and it cannot be refused. It is their prerogative. Since Papa always dressed in shirt and pajamas, I bought these for the Brahmans. Papa also loved wearing rings of different shapes and sizes on his fingers. So I purchased a couple of gold rings weighing three grams each for the Brahmans. Then I kept my fingers crossed, hoping that the Brahmans would gracefully accept the gifts we had bought, and not make exorbitant demands.

My sister's father-in-law who had come for the ceremonies cautioned me saying, 'Those Brahmans will ask for the sky. But don't capitulate to their demands.' We decided that whenever a Brahman made a demand, he would signal to me whether to say 'yes' or 'no'. If they were insistent, we would tell them that we needed time to think it over. In this way, we would bring them down.

I gave the Brahmans the gold rings. There were other assorted gifts we got for them, like umbrellas and bed sheets and chappals. They pocketed these things, and then asked us for a bicycle and ten thousand rupees. I was about to give in, when my sister's father-in-law gestured to me to say 'no'. My learning came to my rescue again. I told the Brahmans that while they had a right to ask for gifts, as a kinnar, I had the right to ask for the gifts back. So I would give them the bicycle, but then ask for it back. I had proved too clever for the Brahmans. In the end, they took the gifts and the money we offered them and left.

Finally, we returned to Mumbai. The house seemed so empty without Papa, though friends and relatives kept visiting us. Slowly, life returned to its humdrum routine. Little Anshuman, Shashi's son, who missed Papa at first, now seemed to have forgotten him and went back to his games. My mother took the longest to recover. Attending to my father night and day for the past one year or so, she now had virtually nothing to do and found the day dragging. Little Anshuman was the only one who kept her somewhat occupied.

Nineteen

After *Bigg Boss*, my relations with Lataguru were completely strained. She thought I had made millions on the show and some of that lucre was rightfully hers. She asked for two lakh rupees, and when I told her that I couldn't pay her that much, she verbally abused me. I decided to dump Lataguru.

It was that time of the year when I travelled to Ajmer again. At Ajmer, I heard the news of my own 'murder'! I couldn't believe my ears. Who was responsible for spreading this canard? Could Lataguru be behind it? Actually, it was a hijra named Sonia who was murdered. She lived in Ahmedabad and did sex work. Professional rivalry among hijras who did sex work led to her murder. But now the rumour was that Laxmi was murdered, and it spread like wildfire. Meanwhile, I met my namesake. She was a hijra named Laxmiguru who lived in Delhi.

Nicknamed '*doctrani* guru' by her friends, she was once a brilliant medical student. But tormented by the ragging she experienced in her final year at college, she gave up her education and became a hijra. I had heard about Laxmiguru, but not met her. Now, when we met, we found that we were on the same wavelength. Both of us spoke English, were articulate, and had been to college. This was what differentiated us from other hijras. Laxmiguru invited me to Delhi and I went. She asked if I would be her chela. I said I needed time to think it over. I consulted my friends Kamini and Jumman in Delhi, and they had good things to say about Laxmiguru. As I had dumped Lataguru and was without a guru at the moment, I decided to become Laxmiguru's chela. She was not just my guru, she was my doctrani guru.

Laxmiguru did not insist that I should live with her in Delhi. Because she was educated, she was liberal and democratic. Whenever I went to Delhi, I stayed with her. At such times, she cooked a lot of fish and we would sit down to a hearty meal.

But it wasn't going to be easy for me to escape the tentacles of Lataguru. She complained about me to Lata Nayak, and I was forced to part with the two lakh rupees that she demanded. As if that wasn't enough, I was forced to gift her my chela Kiran's Thane house, which the latter had transferred in my name. The bitch was money-minded to the core.

My head spun. I tried to empathize with Lataguru. Perhaps the wretched life that hijras live had dehumanized her. She couldn't be blamed.

⁓⁓⁓

People are curious to know about hijras. How do we live? Behave? What do we do? Do we kidnap children? What funeral rites are performed for a hijra after her death? Is she cremated or buried? Such questions do not have answers. Only scholars can answer these questions. Because we hijras are so secretive about our lives, hearsay rules the roost.

As hijras, we live ordinary lives, like everyone else. Like the underdog, we are respected by nobody. Except for the newly introduced Aadhaar Card, we have no *aadhaar* or official recognition, or support from any quarter whatsoever. We are thus destitute. Estranged from family and ostracized by society, people couldn't care less how we earn a livelihood, or where our next meal comes from. If a hijra commits a crime, the mob rushes to beat her up, while the police are only too glad to press charges against us. This is not to justify crime, but to reiterate that all crimes have a social dimension, and in the case of hijras, this cannot be overlooked. Yet, it is never taken into account.

We hijras live in ghettoes. In Mumbai and Thane, many such ghettoes exist in neighbourhoods like Dharavi, Ghatkopar, Bhandup, Byculla, and Malad. The eviction of the poor from the city takes its toll on the ghettoes. They begin to shrink in size. The hijras then disperse towards townships, like Navi Mumbai, where survival is a bit easier.

Our main occupation is to perform badhai at weddings or when a child is born. But can badhai alone fill our stomachs? Obviously not, and so we supplement our earnings by begging on city streets and going to the shops. We also do sex work and dance in bars and night clubs. Dancing comes naturally to us hijras.

It is believed that all hijras are castrated. We call it 'Nirvana'. In the eyes of the public, we are castrated males. But that is not always the case. Castration is strictly optional, and every hijra decides for herself whether or not to undergo it. Castration cannot be forced upon a hijra. Though the world believes that a castrated hijra alone is a *real* hijra, we do not endorse this. I am not castrated. I did not opt for it and my guru did not pressure me into it. Most of my chelas are also uncastrated like me. But yes, many of us have had breast implants. The surgery is expensive, but without it, our transformation is incomplete. However, unlike many other hijras, I haven't gone for hormone therapy in my desire to look feminine. Though I am not castrated, the hijras regard me as one of them.

At times, we hijras are in the news for the wrong reasons. Say, for kidnapping a child and forcing it to become a hijra. Here, what is needed is unbiased and impartial inquiry. Prejudice shouldn't dominate. That hijras receive orders from their community to convert people to their gender is a myth. Our elders have never advised us to force someone to become a hijra. The decision to become a hijra is traumatic. Once one becomes a hijra, the doors to one's earlier life are shut for ever. It isn't easy for a hijra to come to terms with her new life. The family, and indeed society as a whole, reacts strangely. Terrified, the hijra in self-defence invents the story of her having gotten kidnapped and forced into hijrahood. Sometimes, even a complaint to that effect is lodged. Of course, it's not as if hijras *never* kidnap kids. But then the community doesn't forgive them. Like mainstream society, the hijra community, too, has its share of black sheep. Though the laws of the land should be sufficient to deal with them, crimes by hijras are often exaggerated and the hijras are chastised. Disproportionate punishment is meted out to us by the police and the public. This is unfair.

Yet another myth about us is that the funeral of a hijra is performed late in the night and she is beaten with slippers. The unearthly hour is chosen, it is said, so that none should witness the funeral. But this is rubbish. Hijras belong to different religions, and our last rites depend on our religion. A hijra who is a Hindu is cremated, while a Muslim hijra is buried. When carrying the corpse of a dead hijra to the graveyard, we shed our women's clothing and dress instead in shirt and pant, or in kurta and pajama. We do this to hide the fact that the deceased is a hijra.

The hijras are a family. The guru is the mother. Then there's the *dadguru* who is the grandmother, and the *purdahguru* who is the great grandmother. The guru and her chelas comprise a family. A guru selects a successor and trains her. If a guru fails to choose a successor, the *panch*, or the leaders of the seven hijra gharanas, choose her. All crucial decisions are made by the panch. Its leaders are wise ones who command the respect of the entire community.

Once one decides to become a hijra, there is a christening ceremony, the reet, which she must undergo. It is a bit like the *janwa* or thread ceremony of the

Brahmans. The rites are performed by the guru and the disciple is initiated. The charter of rules and regulations is explained to the aspirant. These concern everyday things like how a hijra must walk, and how she must serve water to a visitor. While serving water, the glass must not be held at the top or the middle. Instead, the glass must be balanced on palms joined together. The *pallu* of the hijra's sari mustn't touch anyone as she moves around. One should not lie with one's feet facing the guru. The guru's clothes mustn't be worn by the chela, nor should she utter her guru's or gharana's name. The hijra should not talk back to her guru. And so on.

There is a saying among us that for a hijra, it is all words and nothing else. Guru is a word. Chela is a word. The woman in the guru makes her feel motherly towards her chelas, but the man in the guru makes her authoritarian and dictatorial.

In everyday life, we do not observe the rules of our community that strictly. But we do when our leaders are around. This is just as it is in mainstream society. At the end of the day, it all depends on how liberal (or otherwise) your guru is.

My guru never imposed restrictions on me. However, Lataguru did not want me to talk about my life to the press, or allow them to publish my photographs. At first,

I observed all the rules because the decision to become a hijra was, after all, mine. But soon there came a time when I rebelled. I could not stand the restrictions on my freedom. I began to give interviews to the media. I appeared on television. I travelled abroad. I drank liquor. The community fined me for these transgressions. I paid the fine and committed the 'offences' again. I was all but ostracized by the community. But my chelas stood by me. They were proud of me because I was educated and had a mind of my own. So what if I broke all the rules?

It is tiresome to swim against the current. I have been swimming against two currents—one society and the other community. Both need to change their attitude. Whereas society needs to confront its biases towards the hijras, the hijras themselves must be forthright. We have paid a hefty price for living an estranged and secluded life. The black sheep in the community, no more than ten per cent of our total population, defame the entire community.

To counter this defamation, I have recently established a support group known as the Maharashtra Trutiya Panthi Sanghatana (MTPS). We fight for the fundamental rights of hijras. We managed to persuade the state government and the Planning Commission to give us the Aadhaar Card. Since hijra sex workers are susceptible to HIV and

AIDS, we work towards the eradication of these diseases. We try to obtain housing and employment for the hijras. Change is only possible when the laws change. And for that the authorities need to be approached. It is happening in other Indian states, so why not here, in Maharashtra? In Tamil Nadu, the hijras have been given houses. In Madhya Pradesh, they have stood for elections and won. The hijras have potential. Their families must support them so that they realize their potential.

The tireless efforts of the MTPS bore fruit. The Maharashtra government decided to include transgenders in their special policy for women. I was in my hometown in Uttar Pradesh when I got a call from Samyukta, an activist-associate. 'There is a meeting on 29 November at the Sahyadri Guest House in Mumbai,' Samyukta said. 'Members of the Women's Commission in Delhi will be attending the meeting. Special provisions are to be made for third-gender persons. You've got to be there.' I told Samyukta that I was at my native place and would not be able to return by the 29th. This was before my father's death, and we had gone to Uttar Pradesh to have the *Bhagwat*, a religious scripture, read in our house, as per Papa's wish. My mother, Shashi, Sapna, and Anshuman travelled with us. But Samyukta was not prepared to hear excuses. 'Well, you have to attend the meeting and that's that,' she said before hanging up.

I knew at that moment that I *had* to attend the meeting, come what may. A meeting at the Sahyadri Guest House at Walkeshwar, which was the chief minister's office-cum-residence, was no small thing. My mother and I bought tatkal train tickets, and I returned to Mumbai in time for the meeting.

When I arrived at the Sahyadri Guest House, I found that the meeting had already begun. Varsha Gaikwad, Minister for Women and Child Development, was on the dais. When she saw me enter, she referred to me by name and welcomed me. I was pleasantly surprised. I did not know that I had become so famous that a minister knew me by name! I sat down, listened carefully to Varsha Gaikwad's speech, took notes, and then, during question hour, raised points. Some people in the audience seemed uncomfortable with what I said, but Varsha Gaikwad was herself assuring me that women and third-gender persons, who were sexually exploited, were the responsibility of the government.

Before the meeting was over, we formed expert subcommittees that would look into issues that concerned the hijras. Several scholars and social workers were on these committees. One of our recommendations was that conditions be made more favourable and congenial in schools, so that third-gender kids did not abandon their studies for fear of being ridiculed. For this, the teaching and non-teaching staff that ran the schools would have to be sensitized. Workshops would have to be conducted to make them understand that third-gender children are children with special needs. As adults, third-gender persons had to have access to all documents like a passport, a ration card, and an Aadhaar Card that would help them establish their identity, so that they were not 'missing persons' or their country's lost property. New laws had to be introduced to make sure that we were not discriminated against when it came to things like health care and admission to hospitals.

Our recommendations washed with the honourable minister, who in turn presented them to the chief minister. The chief minister gave all of us Certificates of Appreciation.

I was the first hijra in the world to receive a Certificate of Appreciation from the chief minister.

Twenty

Subhadra was my very first chela. She was murdered at Sheelfata. Many of my other chelas have passed away. Kiran succumbed to AIDS. She loved me selflessly. She was intelligent and disciplined, and had terrific managerial skills. Rupa, who was a fashion designer, also died of AIDS. Payal was a wonderful cook. *Kanda poha*, Spanish omlette, and chicken biryani were her specialty. But she took to excessive drinking and died of alcoholism.

I try to save hijras like Kiran, Rupa, and Payal. I talk them out of their vices. But in my heart of hearts I know that words are poor consolation. As a hijra myself, I can empathize with their anguish. The female psyche, trapped in a male body, stifles them. There's no one in this world they can truly call their own. They don't have an easy means of livelihood. Their sex work results in mental pressure and anxiety, and nagging questions about their identity. Their working conditions are gruesome. A hijra often thinks to herself: *Saala, what is this life*! And to blot out her misery, makes liquor her best friend. But this association proves costly. It eats into one's vitality. I thus failed to save the lives of Rupa, Kiran, and Payal.

And Shahin. No one who saw her would call her a hijra. She was a Bollywood heroine! She nursed the sick like Florence Nightingale! When my father was dying, I entrusted him to her. She would buy medicines from the store downstairs and give them to him at the prescribed time. She stood by my mother and brother Shashi like a pillar of strength.

Shahin was Shahid Naik before her christening. He was born after his eldest sister. They belonged to the Konkan. When Shahid was ten, his mother died and he was brought up by his grandfather in Mumbra, Mumbai. As a child, he was fond of household chores. He helped his mother in the kitchen. Though his mother was touched by his concern, the others in the house pooh-poohed him. They called him names. They thought he was girlish. When Shahid grew up, he befriended some homosexual men. That's how I got to know him. He wanted to become a hijra, but he wasn't old enough to be initiated. So I advised him not to convert just yet, but to hang out with us and finish college. But Shahid was adamant. He began to live like a hijra in the company of Subhadra and Sangita. One fine day, Shahid Naik became Shahin. Became my chela. Her family had no clue. They thought she was out shooting for a film because that is what she told them when she left home. Shahin never went home after that.

One day, Shahin received a call from her uncle. He wanted to meet her. A meeting was arranged, and when the family saw her in a sari they began to wail hysterically. They wanted her to get back into men's clothes and return home. But Shahin meant business. She stayed with us and earned money.

When Shahin's younger sister got married, it was Shahin who bore the expenses. The family then took her back into the fold. Today, Shahin's father is in touch with her. When Shahin goes home on annual visits, she takes gifts for everyone. Her brother refused to speak to her at first, but relented later. Only her stepmother hasn't come round yet.

Then there's Kamal. He was the only son of an Ulhasnagar (Mumbai) businessman. But from childhood, he was fond of cross-dressing: wearing a sari and make-up. The family dismissed this as a kid's fancy. But one day,

Kamal told his family, 'I will not be able to live as you want me to, as a male.' Saying this, he left home. His best friends were Shiba and Winnie, and all three of them became my chelas.

Kamal's folks landed up at my place in Thane. They were comforted to learn that their only son was safe and sound, and that we lived together as a family. Today, Kamal's folks have opened their doors to her. Sometimes she goes home on overnight jaunts. She's not in the family business, of course, but works in a dance bar. She hands over her earnings to her folks, believing it to be her duty, though her parents are well-off and do not need her money.

There's a family I'm related to by blood, and then there are my chelas who are my other family. I need both families and cannot envisage a life without either.

And so it is that I live with both these families simultaneously. There are two houses on the same floor in the same building. Only a wall separates them. In one house, my mother, my brother Shashi and his wife, and their son Anshuman live. In the other, I live with my chelas. The doors of both houses are kept open all day. People freely move from one house to the other. If my mother is cooking and she suddenly runs out of something, say *besan*, she walks into our kitchen and helps herself to it. Likewise, if Kamal is in need of ginger to put into our tea and does not have it, she borrows it from my mother. As for little Anshuman, he has the best of both worlds, cuddling up in his mother's bed sometimes, and sleeping with me, his *Bade Papa*, in my air-conditioned bedroom, wrapped in a blanket, at other times. My mother gets on well with all my chelas, and they in turn respect her and shower their love on Anshuman.

It is an extraordinary arrangement and neighbours are amazed to see how we've made it work. Others ask how our building society has not objected to a bunch of hijras living in the building. The fact is that some residents did whine in the beginning, especially as some of us worked as bar dancers. When Lataguru lived with us, her outspokenness, too, upset people. But then we decided to be as accommodating as we could, and live with the residents of the building in a spirit of neighbourliness. That softened them. Today, they have grown used to seeing us around and miss us when we are not there.

I have good karma. Millions of people all over the world are not even blessed with one family, whereas I have two. God is great.

I am a hijra and have been accepted by my family. This is rare in a culture where deviant sexuality is enough for parents to disown their offspring. Some hijras are initially kicked out by their families, and later welcomed when they start earning and sending them money. The money is often earned through sex work, but the parents have no qualms in accepting it. Doesn't this amount to pimping one's daughters?

When I was young, I had an inferiority complex and society was responsible for it. But now I have a superiority complex. I have travelled all over the world. I have hobnobbed with the high and mighty. Films have been made on my life. Who can deny that I am a celebrity? People laughed at me once, but today I have the last laugh. But then, I owe all this to my decision to become a hijra. It was a bold decision and it yielded rewards. Had I not become a hijra, I might have been any ordinary effeminate homosexual guy. Being a hijra made me glamorous and militant. At first, I seemed a stranger to myself. But over time, the timid, shy Laxminarayan of old, faded out of existence, and the Laxmi you see before you, aggressive, ready to fight the world, stood in his place.

I do not regret my decision to become a hijra.

But then, it's not as if I don't miss my old self either. I covered my face with a mask till the mask became my skin. And yet there are times when I want to rip off that mask and feel the tenderness of my skin, as it naturally is. A poem I learnt in school nicely sums it up:

> *Take away this wealth, take back this prestige*
> *Snatch from me my youth*
> *But return to me my childhood*
> *Those paper boats and that rain water.*

Twenty-one

I write this final chapter not as a scholar, but as a practicing hijra with hands-down experience. If scholars differ with some of my facts and interpretations, I am willing to stand corrected.

The word 'hijra' is a term of abuse. Its variants in colloquial language include expressions like number six, number nine, and chakka. The word 'hijra' derives from the Urdu word *'hijar'*. A hijar is a person who has walked out of his tribe or community. Thus, a hijra is one who has left mainstream society, comprising men and women, and joined a community of hijras. But the hijra community isn't a monolith. Its history and culture varies from state to state.

In Urdu, the hijras are also called *khwaja sara*. In Hindi, we're also called kinnar. South Indian languages adopt other terms for hijras. For example, in Telugu we're called *napunsakudu*, and in Tamil, *aravani*, after the well-known Mahabharata story of Lord Krishna and Aravan. Though the nomenclature differs, the concept is the same everywhere. Hijras are born as male children biologically. Psychologically, however, they feel they are female. Sexually, they are attracted not to the opposite sex, but to their own sex. This conflict between their biological, and psychological and sexual identities is borne out by their body language—their gestures, mannerisms, movements, and expressions all belong to girls rather than boys. Their social behaviour, which includes dress, hairstyle, make-up, jewellery, etc., is also that of women. Thus, there's a feeling of entrapment, of being jailed in the wrong body.

When a person's biological and psychological and sexual identities are at odds with each other, he becomes a freak in the eyes of society. Society ostracizes him. Overcome by feelings of isolation, such a person desperately seeks out others like him and bands with them. Together with them, he may decide to get rid of his male sexual organs, either through sex reassignment surgery, or by having another hijra sever his private parts from the rest of his body, without anaesthesia. Together, they may acquire breasts, either through hormone therapy or simply by sporting falsies. That is how hijra communities are formed.

The word hijra is a social and not a biological construct. One cannot be born a hijra, though one can be born a hermaphrodite. A hermaphrodite has both male and female sexual organs at birth, whereas a hijra is always born as a male. Then there is the question of the child's sexual orientation at puberty. Enough has been said about this by now for us to know that this is determined by one's X and Y chromosomes. I do not have to add to the body of knowledge that already exists and give my readers a biology lesson.

However, there are some things about hijras that readers may not know. While most hijras tend to be born males, with abnormally low levels of the male hormone testosterone, there are some who are born females, with abnormally low levels of the female hormone oestrogen. Of course, the term hijra, which is a social construct, is not used for such women. They are derogatorily referred to as tomboys or butch females. As far as their sexuality is concerned, they are also homosexual. (The term 'homosexual' is generic and can be used for both males and females.) Yet, male being the empowered sex, a tomboy or butch female can carry herself about with relative ease and without the fear of ridicule, as compared to an effeminate man who has indignities heaped on him. In her case, it may even be seen as a feminist statement.

We hijras virtually have a parallel social structure. There are seven hijra gharanas. These are: Bhendibazaarwala, Bulakwala, Lalanwala, Lucknowwala, Poonawala, Dilliwala, and Hadir Ibrahimwala. Each gharana has a chief, known as nayak. Below the nayak is the guru. A hijra is obliged to observe the laws framed by our nayaks and gurus. We're fined—and even excommunicated—if we fail to observe these laws. The laws, of course, vary from one gharana to another. The outside world is not supposed to know what these laws are. Twice a year we hold our panchayat (court). It is made up of the nayaks of all the seven gharanas. The panchayat hears cases concerning hijra indiscipline and decides on the quantum of punishment to be meted out. If a hijra cannot get along with her guru, she is free to become the chela of another guru from another gharana. But for this, her ex-guru must first be paid a fine. A person who decides to become a hijra must find a guru to perform her initiation rite or reet. The guru then becomes the hijra's mother, and she, the chela, becomes the guru's daughter. By this logic, the guru's other chelas become the hijra's sisters, the guru's sisters become her aunts or massis, and the guru's guru becomes her nani or grandmother. It is a vast extended family.

During a hijra's reet, a dupatta of a particular colour is put on her head. The colour varies from one gharana to another. She is also given a sari. These are symbolic things, after which the hijra's training begins. The training is for survival. The hijra is told to isolate herself from mainstream society. She is taught how to clap with her palms pressed together to create a firecracker-like sound, how to beg, and how to flatter. She is also taught how to harass in order to extract money. This is the hijra's revenge on society for ostracizing her.

I have already pointed out that castration isn't compulsory for a hijra. There are those who believe that one isn't a true hijra unless one is castrated. But they are in the minority. The traditional castration rite is performed on a hijra by another hijra (or dai, or priest) without the use of anaesthesia. It is excruciatingly painful. The genitals must be severed from the hijra's body in one fell stroke. Some say that the hijra must be in the standing position when the castration is done, but others say she must lie on her back. Nowadays, hijras are also allowed to have their castration done in a clinic by a doctor. At first, this was illegal, and doctors did it secretly. Today, however, it is done more openly. Castration is a spiritual process. One has to be ready for it. It cannot be imposed.

After castration, the wound takes about forty days to heal. Hijras believe that they shouldn't use artificial means to stop the blood from flowing. Instead, they should let the blood ooze because this, after all, is male blood that must be allowed to drain away. Only then can female blood enter the hijra's body. After castration, a hijra is not allowed to see a man or woman for forty days.

Castration is followed by another ritual known as *haldi-mehndi*. Here, turmeric is applied to the hijra's face, hands, and feet. A bindi is stuck on her forehead and she is given sugar to eat. Then currency notes are circled around the hijra's head and given away to the poor. This is meant to protect the hijra from the evil eye.

The final rite is a bit strange. It is called *chatala*. The hijra is bathed and dressed in green—green sari, green blouse, and green bangles. Then she is given a jug of milk filled to the brim to pour into the sea. But that is not all. She must show her private part—minus her penis and testicles—to the sea, as she must to a black dog and a leafy tree.

These are broadly the rituals associated with castration, though the different gharanas have the freedom to modify the rituals somewhat to suit their convenience.

When a hijra dies, an artificial penis made of cotton or wheat flour is stuck on her body before she is burnt or buried. This, in order not to forget, that the hijra in question was born as a male.

The goddess that all hijras worship is Bahuchara Mata or Murgiwali Devi. She rides a cock, hence the name Murgiwali Devi. There are various legends bout her.

According to one legend, Bariya, a king of Champaner, was childless. Bahuchara Mata, who was riding a cock, appeared in his dream and said, 'My blessings will give you a son. But for his survival, you must wear a green sari and get castrated.' Another legend has it that a princess was married to a prince from another dynasty, who was effeminate. He would run away to the forest whenever it was time for sex. This went on for a long time. Finally, Bahuchara Mata appeared in the form of the princess and cut off her husband's penis. A third legend speaks of a man who raped a goddess disguised as a woman. The goddess cursed that he would become a eunuch. When he begged the goddess to revoke the curse, the goddess told him that the curse would only be withdrawn if he went to a forest and lived a woman's life there.

The Ramayana and the Mahabharata, India's star epics, have many stories about hijras. The *Kamasutra*, that ancient Indian treatise on sex, also constantly refers to the 'third gender'.

The hijras are also devotees of Lord Shiva in his avatar as Ardhanarishwara, where he combines the male and female elements of Shiva and Parvati, and Purusha and Prakriti.

During the reign of the Mughal emperor Aurangzeb, castration was forbidden. Those who wanted to be castrated had to do so secretly. Since Hinduism permitted castration, while Islam did not, Aurangzeb is said to have forcibly converted many Hindu hijras to Islam.

Hijras were an integral part of the courtly traditions of Muslim kings. But when they were overthrown by the British, the hijras landed on the street. Today, hijras beg in shops and other public places, and do sex work, not out of choice, but out of necessity. How, otherwise, can we keep body and soul together?

The aggressive body language of hijras scares people off, but it is something we have cultivated as a survival tactic. People often throw a few rupees our way, not because they are charitable, but only to get rid of us. A man or a woman surrounded by a group of hijras asking for money is embarrassed to the core, and will do anything to regain his self-respect, even if it means parting with cash. We know this and play on the gullibility of people.

We are expert psychologists.

Seeing what a lucrative business begging can be, some men don saris and pretend to be hijras. The people are easily fooled. There's no telling who is a real hijra and who is faking it. The streets of Mumbai are full of such bogus hijras.

Hijras first earned their right to vote in 1994 in Tamil Nadu. Hijras in Tamil Nadu are allowed to use ladies' toilets. Among Indian states, Tamil Nadu is the state that has done the most for the welfare of the hijras. This is possibly because a large number of hijras come from Tamil Nadu.

The hijras even have their own politician. She is Shabnam Mausi who was elected, in 1998, to the state legislative assembly in Madhya Pradesh from the Suhagpur constituency. As a child, Shabnam Mausi studied only up to the second standard. Yet, she was widely travelled and spoke twelve languages, and this is what motivated her to stand for elections and win. Another hijra, Kamal Jan, was elected as mayor of Katni city, again in Madhya Pradesh, in the year 2000. Simultaneously, Asha Devi was also elected mayor of Gorakhpur, Uttar Pradesh. Shabnam Mausi even founded her own political party. She called it Jiti Jitayi Politics.

Hijras are referred to as transgender. To me, the term transgender means 'transcending gender'. In the formulation 'LGBT', ours is the only category that refers to gender. All the other three categories—lesbian, gay, and bisexual—refer to sexuality. I have read somewhere that the terms 'homosexual' and 'heterosexual' are now becoming redundant. They are coming to be replaced by the terms 'andro-sexual' for those who are attracted to men and 'gyno-sexual' for those who are attracted to women.

I have also heard of feminists who are against transgender people. They argue that although we feel we are women, there is a huge difference between *feeling* that one is a woman and actually *being* a woman. According to them, it is only a woman who knows what the female body is, and it is only a woman who can conceive and give birth to a child.

Afterword

*H*ijras are a despised lot in India. The average Indian thinks of hijras as a menace and a nuisance, and runs away on spotting them on the streets. This bias, or worse, prejudice towards hijras is shared by both men and women alike. Men are shamed and embarrassed when surrounded by a group of hijras who stubbornly beg for money, refusing to let go till the person concerned parts with at least a few rupees. This money is not necessarily given out of a sense of sympathy or charity, but simply to get rid of the creature that has made one its 'victim', often to the amusement of others present. Frequently, the person's ordeal does not end, in spite of his having given away his hard-earned money to the hijra. If the hijra thinks that the amount given is too measly, she and her friends may pester the giver for more, resorting to obscene language and gestures to torment him further. A friend of mine who lives in suburban Mumbai and commutes to work in the city's Central Business District by local train every morning, once told me that he always set out from home with prayer on his lips: that he should not be caught in the clutches of a hijra; if that unfortunately happened, his whole day was screwed up. Women commuters who travel in the ladies compartments of Mumbai's local trains recall harrowing tales of being harassed by hijras, not just for money, but also for seats in the overcrowded cars. There have been occasions when these hapless women have been driven to tears by the antics of a band of hijras, and have had no one to turn to for succour. 'Men who molest us in public spaces can be dealt with by a simple thing like a slap,' a woman commuter was telling me, 'or by reporting the matter to the police. But with hijras it is different. We would make a laughing stock of ourselves if we either slapped them or took them to the police. The hijras know this, and that's how they get away.' Bollywood films, by continually stereotyping hijras, as indeed they do every marginalized section of society, only add to our jaundiced view of them. Rarely has Bollywood come up with a sensitive portrayal of a hijra, a notable exception being Pooja Bhatt's film *Tamanna*. Hijras do not want to be nice. They grow up with a sense of being wronged by

Nature, and their method of redressing or righting this wrong is by taking it out on 'normal' men and women, towards whom Nature has been partial. Their behaviour on the streets is thus subversive. We of the mainstream only know hijras by their behaviour on the streets. We hardly know anything about them besides the fact that they beg, sing, and dance. In addition, there are several myths about hijras in circulation that act to their detriment. One such myth is that hijras kidnap young male children, castrate them, and forcibly make them hijras.

Laxmi's autobiography is one of the earliest works that belong to the genre of hijra literature. It seeks to make readers aware of who the hijras really are, and what goes into the shaping of their personalities—yes, they do have personalities. It seeks to dispel myths about the hijras and help us shed our prejudices. One of Laxmi's primary endeavours is to show us that hijras are ordinary people, no different from us: they do not exist in a rarefied realm. And yet, Laxmi's autobiography must not be read in isolation, as a one-off text. Instead, it must be placed within the wider tradition of Lesbian-Gay-Bisexual-Transgender (LGBT) writing in India. Non-heterosexual people have been writing testimonies about their lives and loves for hundreds, if not thousands, of years. In their seminal text *Same Sex Love in India*, Ruth Vanita and Saleem Kidwai give us samples of this writing from different historical periods, which they classify as ancient, medieval, and modern. The earliest writing involves mythological rather than real people, and Devdutt Pattanaik joins Vanita and Kidwai here to reinterpret mythological tales from a non-heterosexual perspective in books like *Shikhandi and Other Tales They Don't Tell You*, *The Pregnant King*, and several others. In *Sakhiyani*, Giti Thadani writes about lesbian sculptures in ancient Indian temples, like the temples of Khajuraho and Konark. But the real testimonies, of flesh-and-blood people, begin from the Middle Ages onwards and are written in languages like Persian and Urdu, and, later, in many region-specific Indian languages, and in English.

In modern India, one can randomly speak of Ismat Chughtai's story '*Lihaaf*' (written originally in Urdu and translated into English as *The Quilt*), of Suniti Namjoshi's many poems and fiction such as *Feminist Fables* and *The Conversations of Cow*, of the poetry of Sultan Padamsee, and of Aubrey Menen's autobiographical books *The Space within the Heart* and *It Is All Right*. The next generation of writers would include Vikram Seth, whose poems in *The Humble Administrator's Garden* and *The Golden Gate* comprise several poems on the theme of same-sex longing. Many of Mahesh Dattani's plays, like *A Muggy Night in Mumbai* and *Night Queen*, are on the theme of homosexual identity, while the poems of Aga Shahid Ali explore the notion of gay love in a veiled and circumspect way. But the most prolific gay writer of twentieth-century India is, undoubtedly, Hoshang Merchant, with over 25 collections of gay poetry to his credit, as well as the startling autobiography *The Man Who Would Be Queen*.

LGBT anthologies and compilations of gay and lesbian testimonies by Indians, and by people of Indian origin, have been in circulation since the 1980s, as Rakesh Ratti's *A Lotus of Another Color*, Hoshang Merchant's *Yaraana*, Ashwini Sukthankar's *Facing the Mirror*, Gautam Bhan and Arvind Narrain's *Because I Have a Voice*, and Minal Hajratwala's *Out* demonstrate.

Gay scholarship, too, has been quick to keep pace with the changing trends. Ruth Vanita's *Queering India* and *Love's Rite*, Parmesh Shahani's *Gay Bombay*, submitted to Massachusetts Institute of Technology, USA, for a PhD degree, Hoshang Merchant's *Forbidden Sex/Forbidden Text*, and Brinda Bose and Subhabrata Bhattacharya's edited book *The Phobic and the Erotic* are important works in this regard.

My own work has been consistently queer since I published my first collection of short stories, *One Day I*

Locked My Flat in Soul City, in 1995. After that, there was no looking back. In 1996, Riyad Wadia chose six poems from my work-in-progress poetry collection, *BomGay*, and converted them into a chic 11-minute short film, with actor Rahul Bose in the lead. (The collection, made up of some 26 poems, finally came out as a chapbook in 2006.) That same year (1996), I published my collection of plays titled *The Wisest Fool on Earth and Other Plays*. The title play, a gay monologue spoken from a washroom in a Bombay high-rise, was performed in English in Bombay and Pune, and, later, in Hindi in Hyderabad. In 2001, *One Day I Locked My Flat in Soul City* was reissued with more gay stories in it (the book may be reissued again this year or early next year with still more gay and lesbian stories in it). Meanwhile, an Italian edition of the book appeared in 2010. But my most overtly gay novel, *The Boyfriend*, which many reviewers called India's first full-fledged gay novel, came out in 2003. The book, still in print, is in its twentieth edition, and has been translated into French and Italian; it has also been optioned for an art house film by a Bombay-based movie director. In 2009, I co-edited *Whistling in the Dark* with my former student Dibyajyoti Sarma: the work comprised interviews with 21 queer persons from different sections of society and of different nationalities. The following year (2010), my second overtly gay novel, *Hostel Room 131* came out, and later this year, my third overtly gay novel, *Lady Lolita's Lover*, is likely to see the light of day. In between, in 2012, Poetrywala, Bombay, published my new and selected poems in a slim volume titled *For Hire*, in which several poems were about same-sex desire.

The tradition of gay writing in India continues, with newer (and younger) writers like Siddharth Dhanvant Shanghvi, Mahesh Natarajan, and Himadri Roy adding to the impressive body of work that already exists. Though most of the writing inventoried above is in English, some of it is also in regional languages like Marathi and Tamil. In Marathi, Bindumadhav Khire's two books, *Partner* and *Indradhanush*, and the late Chetan Datar's *Ek Madhav Baug* deserve mention, along with plays like Pramod Kale's *Na Yetil Uttare* and Zameer Kamble's *Hijra*. In Tamil, on the other hand, Revathi's *The Truth about Me: A Hijra Life Story* (translated into English by V. Geetha) is the one work that comes closest to Laxmi's, and is, in fact, its precursor. This is because Revathi, like Laxmi, is also a hijra, and her book, like Laxmi's, is also an autobiography. At the same time, the two books are very different.

Revathi's account of her life is, what I would call, essentialist. Laxmi's account, conversely, is anti-essentialist.

These terms are illuminatingly used by the queer theorist Jonathan Dollimore, in his book *Sexual Dissidence*, to highlight the difference between two nineteenth-century European writers, André Gide and Oscar Wilde. Both Gide and Wilde were homosexual men, but while Gide was a devout Protestant whose religion was in conflict with his homosexuality, which he regarded as his essential identity, Wilde regarded himself as a sexual transgressor who did not possess any essential identity. Revathi, likewise, derives her essential identity by virtue of her being a hijra. Laxmi, conversely, de-centres through her being, the very idea of an essential identity. Thus, Revathi consistently portrays herself as a victim, whereas Laxmi's endeavour seems to be to show that, in spite of being a hijra, she is *not* a victim. On the face of it, Revathi's is the more controlled and gripping story. Not once does she stray from her chosen course, which is to depict the humiliation and violence that hijras face on a daily basis, as a result of which her book is unputdownable. Laxmi also speaks of humiliation, but it is restricted to the early part of her narrative, when she is still a boy. Once she becomes a hijra, Laxmi, unlike Revathi, begins to live life on her own terms. She becomes an activist, works for the eradication of AIDS among her people, and attends national and international conferences. She can put her own story on hold to insert an aside about her pet dog!

Laxmi has supportive parents who come to terms with her status as a hijra. The backing of her parents and family members insulates her from the taunts of the world, and though she talks about the terrible things that happen to other hijras, including to some of her own chelas, none of these things ever happen to her. Laxmi's parents even appear with her on TV and state that they are proud of their daughter, that they'd much rather accept her as a hijra than leave her on the streets to beg and trade her body. Revathi, by contrast, has parents and brothers who come across as brutes. There are constant property disputes in the family, and Revathi is given virtually no share of the property, which is her punishment for voluntarily relinquishing her manhood. At the same time, when Revathi becomes a sex worker, her parents have no qualms about living off her earnings: this makes them out to be pimps who trade their daughter. Apart from her parents and brothers, Revathi has to defer to the wishes of older hijras throughout her life, while Laxmi is able to stand up to bullies like Lataguru when they become a thorn in her flesh.

Then there's the question of sex, and Revathi's book is sensational for her graphic descriptions of sexual activity among the hijras. Sex, so to speak, spills out of every page of *The Truth about Me*. Laxmi studiously avoids any reference to sex in her book, not wanting it, possibly, to be mistaken for a work of pornography. In doing so, however, she also risks being regarded as prudish. In this context, one may point out that Revathi, like most women, had a desire to get married and actually managed to marry a man, though the marriage did not last. Laxmi betrays no desire to get married, and there is no reference to marriage anywhere in her book, though she derives a thrill when she attends her brother Shashinarayan's wedding.

Revathi refers to three of her chelas from Bangalore, one of them being the ravishing Famila, who later committed suicide. Where Revathi was docile and submitted to the tyrannies of the world, the Bangalore hijras were upfront and in-your-face. It was education that was responsible for their difference of approach, and, it must be emphasized here that, at the end of the day, what redeems Laxmi is her education, almost up to the postgraduate level. Because she is college-educated, Laxmi is able to battle (and baffle) the system when it refuses to give her a passport on account of her being a hijra. But here, though Revathi is not college-educated, her story has a striking parallel with Laxmi's, as she goes to get a driver's licence. She is driven from pillar to post at the Regional Transport Office, just as Laxmi is at the passport office, but in the end she comes home with her licence in hand. In their brush with the bureaucracy, the testimonies of all hijras are more or less the same.

Perhaps the biggest difference between Revathi and Laxmi is that while the former is castrated, the latter is not. In Revathi's essentialist account of her life, castration obviously occupies a prominent place in the narrative. Almost five pages of her book are devoted to her own castration, which, in the manner of the Tamil Nadu hijras, she calls her nirvana. Orthodox hijras in Tamil Nadu and elsewhere are required to have their castration rite performed by a *thayamma* in the traditional, ritualistic way, without anaesthesia. The excruciating pain and the bloodletting that is caused as a result is symbolic of the draining away of the hijra's manhood. It is said that when a thayamma performs the rite, she makes sure that the hijra's penis and testicles are severed from her body in one stroke. Loud, ear-splitting music accompanies the rite, and this has the effect of drowning the hijra's screams. But times have changed. Where hijras were compulsorily made to have their nirvana done by a thayamma in the past, Revathi is given a choice and told she can have it done by a doctor; in fact, her nani strongly recommends the latter course. Revathi seems a little unhappy about this, but capitulates in the end, possibly because the torture of the crude thayamma operation terrifies her. Even so, she is still in pain as the effect of the anaesthesia administered to her by her doctor wears off. Readers are liable to get gooseflesh as they pore over her descriptions of how she and another hijra, who also had her nirvana done at the same time, travelled back from Tamil Nadu to Bombay in an unreserved train compartment soon after the surgery, howling in agony throughout the journey. As far as Laxmi is concerned, I would tend to regard the fact that she is not castrated as another instance of her anti-essentialism. Laxmi is self-conscious and evasive about the issue of castration and dismisses it in a few lines in Chapter 19 of her book. She suggests that one has to be emotionally, spiritually, and psychologically ready for castration before one undertakes it. In the early chapters, there is but one passing reference to castration, when she worries that the passport officials may reject her claims to being a hijra by virtue of her not being castrated. Laxmi's character, as brought out by her book, gives us the feeling that, unlike Revathi, she does not have the capacity to suffer pain. She has grown accustomed to the good life, devoid of hardship. The sadomasochism of a castration operation is not for her. The very thought of mutilating her body seems revolting to Laxmi. But there is another issue at stake here, and it is about her relationship with her family. If Laxmi's family, unlike Revathi's, has accepted her, it is on the exclusive condition that she continues to be their *son* at home, though she may be a hijra outside. In such a scenario, her castration would be totally unacceptable to the family. This is proved by the fact that Laxmi's parents disliked her dressing in female attire at home, and insisted that she wear shirts and trousers like her brother. One way to read this is that Laxmi compromised on some of her principles here to enjoy homely comforts and the warmth of family life. Another reading would be that there are residues of male privilege in Laxmi that she is unwilling to let go, as it were, by clinging to her genitals. By contrast, Revathi is homeless throughout her life. The thing that seems to irk her parents and brothers the most is that she has 'chopped off her cock'. Perhaps, Revathi would have earned the sympathy of her family if, like Laxmi, she did not have her nirvana done. In patriarchal cultures like ours, where the desire to have sons is so over-abiding that doctors will illegally perform ultrasound tests on expectant mothers to determine the foetus's gender (and abort it if it is that of a girl), the thought of a son voluntarily becoming a daughter is bewildering to parents. It makes them burn in shame and burn with fury. Activists like Ashok Row Kavi have argued that hijras do not opt for castration because a large percentage of their earnings comes from sex work. This prompts many of them to keep their genitals intact so that they can be versatile and cater to all types of customers. Most people imagine that it is heterosexual men who go to hijras to have sex with them, as they do with women. Indeed, Revathi continues to be a sex worker even after her nirvana, and it is such straight men that she services. She talks of men who mistake her to be a woman (including a petrol pump attendant who wanted to marry her), and do not find out till the end that she is a hijra. However, hijras also cater to homosexual men who go to them precisely because they think they are men and not women.

The autobiographies of Laxmi and Revathi reveal that both of them attempted to commit suicide. And, as pointed out above, Famila, one of Revathi's chelas, successfully managed to take her own life. The methods Laxmi and Revathi choose in order to end their lives concern the elements: Laxmi opts for death by drowning during a beach trip to Gujarat with her friends, while Revathi tries to set herself on fire outside her parental home in Tamil Nadu. Both Laxmi and Revathi are saved in the nick of time—Laxmi by her friends, and

Revathi on account of the fact that she could not find a matchstick! This is best described in her own words:

> I poured kerosene over my head and demanded a matchstick from the crowd of onlookers ... My parents and brothers remained inside [the house]. Perhaps they wanted me to set myself on fire and die ... For about fifteen minutes, I stood there, kerosene in my hair, screaming and sobbing in agony ... No one came forward to console me or help me. If I had access to a matchbox I would have surely set myself on fire. But ... there was no matchbox and after a while, I changed my mind. (pp. 253–4)

Neither Laxmi nor Revathi then makes a second attempt to end her life. But they continue to be unhappy, and both of them talk about taking to heavy drinking at home and in bars to cope with their misery. What Famila's suicide and Laxmi's and Revathi's attempts at suicide tell us is that in spite of the popularity they achieved, their lives, in the ultimate analysis, are no different from the lives of ordinary hijras who roam the streets. Mainstream society, as pointed out above, thinks of hijras as a menace. Yet, when it suits us, we think of hijras as mascots who bring good luck to a house in which a marriage has been solemnized or a child has been born. At such times, hijras are sought after for their blessings or badhai. They are invited to sing and dance. But once the festivities are over, they are easily forgotten. They return to lives characterized by ostracism, poverty, humiliation, abuse, brutality, violence, and hate. We deny hijras their basic human rights. We relegate them to the shadows. Hijras thus remain uneducated and disempowered. When hijras beg and solicit on the streets, we are unable to connect that to their hunger pangs because, to us, hijras do not possess stomachs and do not feel hunger. Middle-class India thinks of hijras as extraterrestrials. But when hijras exit mainstream society and join hijra clans, their lives do not always qualitatively improve, as the autobiographies of Laxmi and Revathi so poignantly bring out. However, where the zesty Famila threw in the towel, the mature Laxmi and Revathi picked up the pieces of their lives and began to work for their community. In a way, the journey of both Laxmi and Revathi begins with their attempt at suicide, and ends with social and political activism, as Laxmi first joins the DWS and then sets up Astitva, and Revathi joins Sangama in Bangalore.

As a category, 'hijra' is a social, as opposed to a natural or biological, construct. A hijra is first born as a male and becomes a hijra later. If he castrates himself, he becomes a eunuch. A hijra is different from a hermaphrodite who is naturally born with both male and female sexual organs and characteristics. A hijra may be narrowly defined as one who starts out as an effeminate homosexual man from the lower strata of society who, because of a lack of money and education, believes he can only survive in a community or ghetto of like-bodied and like-minded people. He thus leaves home, exactly, as say, a sadhu does, to become a hijra and never to return to the family and the society on which he has turned his back. He might even come to see his life before he became a hijra as a sort of past life. The words 'effeminate' and 'homosexual' that we have used above need to be analysed. All effeminate men do not become hijras. Similarly, all homosexual men are not hijras, though, as Hoshang Merchant suggests in his introduction to *Yaraana*, the uninitiated may sometimes take them to be so. Many effeminate men from upper-class society deliberately flaunt and exaggerate their effeminacy in order to be 'camp' or 'metrosexual'. Such men may regard themselves as 'transgender' which is a broader term than hijra, the latter category being only a variety of the former. Transgendered men may become transsexuals by opting for sex reassignment (or realignment) surgery, and might choose to describe themselves as trans-women. The surgery itself, carried out in five-star clinics by expensive private surgeons, would hardly be referred to as 'castration'. Unlike a traditional castration operation, it would be marked by intensive post-operative care where the patient is counselled and put through specialized hormonal therapy to make the transition process foolproof. As examples, we may cite the case histories of two well-known Bombay-based trans-women, Farah Rustom (formerly Faroukh Rustom) and Aida Banaji (formerly Adi Banaji). Both came from wealthy Zoroastrian (Parsi) families and lived elite, Westernized lifestyles before and after their transformation, as Riyad Wadia's documentary on the life of Aida Banaji (titled A Mermaid Called Aida) reveals. A crucial difference between such trans-women and hijras seems to be that while the latter voluntarily ghettoize themselves, the former continue to be a part of mainstream society and live life on their own terms. A contrast between these two types of transgender persons is provided in my own novel Hostel Room 131.

A former student of mine, a member of Queer Studies Circle started by me in 1999, let us call him Anirudh, surprised me one day by walking into my office and introducing herself as Anasuya, whom I had not met before. It took me more than a minute to figure out that Anasuya was none other than Anirudh, who, while doing his PhD at a British university, decided to have sex reassignment surgery against the wishes of his parents.

Today, Anasuya teaches sociology in Delhi and lives a fiercely independent life, making me wonder if 'trans-woman' is not an altogether different category from 'hijra', the difference being one, not merely of degree, but also of kind. I recalled, as I spoke to Anasuya, that she was extremely camp even as Anirudh who prided himself on his sexual triumphs (which he saw as conquest). On the other hand, Anirudh/Anasuya never once complained about being sexually abused or exploited.

Perhaps the category that comes closest to 'hijra', and is yet very different from it, is '*koti*', which literally means 'monkey' in Telugu. Men who regard themselves as kotis often come from the same underprivileged sections of society as the hijras. Like hijras, kotis are effeminate in a natural, sincere, and serious, rather than camp, way, and are homosexual. Yet, they wish to be a part of the majority. Accordingly, they dress as men, keep their hair short, may be sport an earring or two, and go out to work (often in blue-collar jobs). What is most significant, however, is that they get married to women, the marriages usually being arranged for them by their families. Kotis, like the majority of Indians, see marriage as a social necessity in which the identity of the 'wife' is socially constructed as one who looks after the house, cooks the food, and brings up the children. The 'husband', on the other hand, goes out to work and enjoys male privileges that make it possible for him to lead a secret homosexual life in the after hours, sometimes for monetary considerations. By thus allowing patriarchy to co-opt them, kotis manage to mainstream themselves, for in the eyes of the world they lead normative, householder lives, while as homosexual men they remain strictly in the closet. Their supposed male supremacy convinces them that they do not have to tell their wives about their homosexuality or bisexuality, and, in turn, the wives too may be co-opted by patriarchy to such an extent that they might not regard their husbands' encounters with other men (if at all they get to know about them) as adultery. Some educated, upwardly mobile homosexuals (like Pratibha Sixer Rani of Bangalore) also regard themselves as kotis, but I would argue that in reality they blend the categories of 'koti' and 'gay' (in the Western sense) because they do not succeed, by virtue of their lifestyles, in completely mainstreaming themselves.

Hijras display a fundamental paradox. While they destabilize normativity on the basis of their gender identity, they also betray a desire for normativity on the basis of their sexuality. It is fairly established by now that (in spite of what some quacks and some holy men of assorted religions dubiously claim, as, for example, in

Benjamin Law's book *Gaysia*), one's sexuality cannot be reversed: a homosexual cannot become a heterosexual, and a heterosexual cannot become a homosexual, even if he wants to. The hijra position seems to be that heterosexuality must be achieved at any cost; if it cannot be achieved through a reversal of sexuality, it must be achieved through a reversal of gender. Thus, hijras, like transsexuals, may be said to become women in order to be able to have sex with the men of the world, in the manner of heterosexuals. The trans-woman Farah Rustom (referred to earlier) is said to have acquired a German lover soon after her transformation, and was peeved by the fact that as a trans-woman she would not be able to conceive and give birth to his child. Laxmi is so convinced that she is a woman that she feels squeamish about having sex with a trans-man whom she meets in the Netherlands, perhaps because that would make her out to be a lesbian, while her endeavour was to become a heterosexual. (A similar situation arises in Amol Palekar's film *Daayra*, where a trans-man falls in love with a trans-woman and the wheel comes full circle as they return to heterosexuality, which they were out to destabilize in the first place.) Because they can afford it, trans-women in the West spend much time and much money attending to every single detail of their transformation (including their pitch), so that no traces of their original selves remain. It is likewise with upper-class transsexuals in India. Aida Banaji, in Riyad's film based on her referred to earlier, speaks of how she wanted to have very large breasts to look the perfect woman, and how, as a consequence, her silica implants messily came off in the taxi as she was on her way home from the hospital. For such transsexuals, if their transformation is not complete in every sense of the term, they would merely be regarded by society as men in drag, rather than as transsexuals. Hijras like Laxmi and Revathi do come across as real women (though Laxmi, as we have seen, is not castrated), but many ordinary hijras, because of slipshod castration methods (attributable to their poverty and illiteracy), continue to retain their male characteristics, such as facial hair and a masculine voice, regardless of whether they are castrated or not: it is this that makes them erotically appealing to both heterosexual as well as homosexual men.

Queer theory, that seeks to go beyond gender (male/female) and sexuality (hetero/homo) binaries would make out a case for the ambivalence of gender and sexuality at the *bodily* level (as opposed to the level of consciousness or allegorical level, as in the Chinese concept of the Yin and the Yang, and in the Hindu idea of Ardhanarishwara). Terry Goldie, in his book

Queersexlife, invents the ultimate prescription for such bodily ambivalence when he writes, 'Receptive anal sex is usually a part of my sexual activity even with women. I have had women use strap-ons and I have used a double-ended dildo, with one end in the woman's vagina and the other in my anus.'

One of Terry Goldie's favourite films is *The Crying Game*, in which Fergus, an IRA volunteer, falls in love with his black friend Jody's black girlfriend Dil (after Jody is killed in an attack), till Dil reveals to Fergus that she has a penis. Dil shoots Fergus's former girlfriend Jude (white, and a real woman) in a fit of jealousy, but it is Fergus rather than Dil who is arrested for Jude's murder, while Dil regularly visits him in jail. The triumph, thus, in the film is of Dil who incorporates the ambivalence principle. National Geographic Channel, in its late-night show *Taboo*, once featured a sex worker, the upper part of whose body was female, and the lower part male: the sex worker was thus in possession of both breasts and a penis and said s/he would do nothing to give up either the one or the other. To Foucault, gayness or queerness (as opposed to mere homosexuality) is a catalyst that dismantles the status quo and heralds change. Mere homosexuality, by contrast, replicates mainstream heterosexuality by a simple act of substitution: the opposite sex partner becomes a same-sex partner here. Rather than dismantling the status quo and triggering revolution, this limply results in heteronormativity being replaced by what Lisa Duggan has called homonormativity.

To the extent that Laxmi is not castrated, she may be said to encompass the ambivalence principle of queer theory. However, in her case, unlike in the case of the examples cited above, this is not intentional, even though I have called her anti-essentialist. There is a fine distinction between wanting to be ambivalent in the ideological sense and wanting, simply, to have the best of both worlds; in Laxmi's case, it seems to be the latter.

In December 2013, the Supreme Court overruled a Delhi High Court judgement of July 2009 that read down Section 377 of the Indian Penal Code that described all forms of non-procreative heterosexual sex as 'unnatural' and 'carnal', making them a criminal offence. Homosexuality, naturally, came under the purview of the section. The section itself was the handiwork of T.B. Macaulay who introduced it in 1869. Thirty-four years before Macaulay came up with his anti-sodomy law, as Section 377 is sometimes called, he also made English education compulsory in India, in response to the then Governor-General Lord William Bentinck's invitation to him to formulate a new education policy. Macaulay's recommendations to Bentinck appeared in a document known as *The Minute on Education*. As I argue in my introduction to *Whistling in the Dark*, both the switch to English and the criminalizing of all forms of non-procreative sexual activity (including, by implication, anal intercourse between husband and wife) stemmed from the same impulse: purism. Macaulay wanted to cleanse England's jewel in the crown of all forms of decadence and licentiousness that had set in over the centuries, be they in relation to language or in relation to sex. In this, he was behaving like a true Victorian.

In the case of the December 2013 judgement, one of the two judges who authored the retrograde verdict was in his last day in office, and was to retire the next day. A few months later, it was time for the Supreme Court to hear a Public Interest Litigation (PIL), filed by the NGO Alliance India, on transgender rights. This time, the bench comprised two other judges, Justice K.S. Radhakrishnan and Justice A.K. Sikri, both of a progressive mindset. The learned judges not only upheld transgender rights, but also recommended that government jobs be reserved for them, just as they are reserved for the backward castes and classes. The judgement, however, though laudable, led to a Catch 22 situation. Given that transgender people regularly had anal intercourse, did it mean that Section 377 of the Indian Penal Code, while still applicable to homosexual men, would not apply to hijras and transsexuals? As I wrote in my weekly column 'Man to Man' in *Pune Mirror*, a tabloid newspaper issued with *The Times of India*, it meant that if a gay man had sex with a transgender person, only the former would be punished. This, in turn, would lead to another complication because it would violate the principle of equality before the law. On the other hand, if the judgement meant that the court was granting transgender people all rights except the right to have (anal) sex because that had already been criminalized by the same court in its earlier judgement, it implied that transgender people would have to remain celibate all their lives! The Supreme Court landed itself in this tangle because, instead of hearing the two petitions together, it heard them separately. The first petition, as explained above, was about the reading down of Section 377 by the Delhi High Court, against which Baba Ramdev (of all people) appealed, saying that the next thing we would ask for is to be allowed to have sex with animals! The second petition was for transgender rights. Though Justices Radhakrishnan and Sikri were modern and liberal in their outlook, their hands were tied. They could not go against the opinion of one of their own colleagues, Justice Singhvi, who authored the 11 December 2013 judgement before retiring from office the next day. Hence, they wrote, 'While dealing with the present issue, we are not concerned with this aforesaid wider meaning of the expression transgender.' The 'aforesaid wider meaning' had, of course, to do with the clubbing of lesbian, gay, and bisexual with transgender, represented by the popular abbreviation LGBT. The latter judgement thus had the effect of driving a wedge within the queer community and destroying our unity. That apart, the judgement, as I argued in my *Pune Mirror* column, had a serious loophole. How was someone like Laxmi, who was not even castrated, to prove that she was a transgender? Transgender, after all, is a psychological rather than a biological state. Kotis and camp gay men could take advantage of this loophole in the law and lead full-fledged homosexual lives, without being affected by Section 377. The misuse of homosexuality for personal gain is not unknown. Gay activist Vikram Doctor once wrote an article in the *Sunday Times*, in which he pointed out that many heterosexual Indian men sought asylum in the West, particularly in the United States, by claiming to be gay. Karan Johar's *Dostana*, as we know, is also on the same theme. Such misuse was most likely when it came to job reservations for transgender people. It could lead to widespread corruption, for all that it would take is a certificate from a doctor or a hospital to say that one is a transgender, and is therefore eligible for a job under the TG quota. The certificate itself could be bought for a fee, as well as by shamelessly aping the dress and body language of transgender persons, often noted for their limp hands and coquettish walk. Similarly, one could attempt to pass off for a hijra by perfecting the unique way in which hijras clap. This is not to trivialize the issue, but to express genuine concern about the business of transgender rights, no doubt a tremendous victory in itself.

About seven years ago, the celebrated writer Salman Rushdie met Laxmi at her Thane (in Mumbai) home to interview her for the book *AIDS Sutra*, a collection of AIDS stories. This is how he describes his visit:

I went to Thane to meet an exceptional hijra named Laxmi, a hijra of extreme articulacy and force of character. By the Talao Pali Lake in Thane, Laxmi, a local star of sorts, did her 'ramp walk' every evening in the old days when she started out. Laxmi is a rarity among hijras; she lives at home, and, to avoid upsetting her parents, dresses as a man when she is with them. They call her by her male name, Laxmikant [sic], or by her family nickname, Raju, and, as a man, she works at home as a bharatnatyam teacher. But when she leaves home, she is Laxmi, and everyone in Thane knows her. She is a voluptuous person with purple-black lips; hard to miss. Her beginnings are not unusual. (pp. 114–15)

Rushdie, a Mumbai boy himself, refers to a sculpture of Ardhanarishwara at the Elephanta Caves, off the coast of Mumbai, which he refers to as 'half-woman god' and a 'double-gendered deity'. On the other hand, he calls the hijras of today 'contemporary gender benders'. Reminiscing about his childhood in Mumbai, when he often saw hijras roam the streets of Marine Drive and elsewhere to beg and dance, he says 'they seemed alien' to him. He does not describe their castration himself, but relies instead on a graphic, though orientalist, account of it provided by John Irving, in his novel *A Son of the Circus*:

A hijra's operation—they use the English word—is performed by other hijras. The patient stares at a portrait of Goddess Bahucharamata; he is advised to bite his own hair, for there's no anaesthetic, although the patient is sedated with alcohol or opium. The surgeon (who is not a surgeon) ties a string around the penis and the testicles in order to get a clean cut—for it is with one cut that both the testicles and the penis are removed. The patient is allowed to bleed freely; it's believed that maleness is a kind of poison, purged by bleeding. No stitches are made; the large, raw area is cauterized with hot oil. As the wound begins to heal, the urethra is kept open by repeated probing. The resultant puckered scar resembles a vagina. (p. 110)

Rushdie quotes John Irving as saying that the hijras are not simply another sex; they are a 'third gender'. (This term, third gender, is often used by Wendy Doniger and Sudhir Kakar in their translation of the Kamasutra, to refer to people who are neither men nor women.) Rushdie next moves to the statistics, and informs us that no more than 60 per cent of Mumbai's hijras are actually castrated, referring to castration, first as the Operation (in the manner of John Irving) and then as Nirvana, which, of course, is what the hijras themselves call it. However, according to him, castration is compulsory for a hijra in Gujarat. Rushdie thinks that Laxmi's claim that there are 1,00,000 hijras in Mumbai alone is an exaggeration. He randomly puts their number at a mere 5,000, and says that 1,00,000 seems 'closer to the total figure for hijras in the whole of India'. Rushdie travels with Laxmi to Kamatipura, Mumbai's infamous red-light area, 'where there is a special hijra alley'. According to him, the hijras of Mumbai once owned the entire red-light area, but had to sell it off in phases, as their *gharanas* grew poor.

Much of what Laxmi says to Salman Rushdie about herself during their conversation is included in her autobiography. Rushdie, who otherwise knows very little about Mumbai's gay community, begins to understand it better in Laxmi's company. Laxmi complains to him that the 'activists are trying to put us inside the MSM culture' and that 'the MSM sector is getting so strong'. 'But,' she reiterates, 'we are not simply MSMs. We are not even simply TGs [transgendered persons]. We are ... hijras. I am carrying a whole culture with me. It's that collective aspect, the hijra culture, that is important. We cannot sacrifice it. We are different.'

Rushdie, who probably hears the term MSM for the first time in his life, explains it in parentheses thus: '(MSM are Men who have Sex with Men, and they are of three kinds: Panthis, who go on top, Kothis [*sic*] who go on the bottom, and Double Deckers, who need no explanation).'

Since Rushdie's piece on Laxmi is essentially for a compilation of AIDS-related stories, it naturally pays lip service to India's AIDS politics, pointing out that 'She [Laxmi] wants to be a voice in the HIV/AIDS campaign ... to help save what she, too, calls "the third gender of India".' He then concludes:

The hijras of Bombay and the rest of India are held to be the community most at risk of HIV infection. There have been improvements in organization, outreach, education and self help, but for many hijras, their lives continue to be characterized by mockery, humiliation, stigmatization, fear, and danger. Laxmi of Thane and the 'peer educators' of Malwani may be success stories, hijras who have taken charge of their destinies and are trying to help their fellows, but many hijras are mired in poverty and sickness. (p. 117)

Mi Hijra, Mi Laxmi has been translated into English by us from the Marathi. It is a collaborative translation, with one of us (P.G. Joshi) working with the Marathi original (the source language) and the other (me) 'Englishing' the narrative (putting it into the target language). However, neither Joshi nor I are completely oblivious of the other's language: Joshi was, till recently, professor of English at a college affiliated to the University of Pune, and I am a domiciled Maharashtrian. What complicates the work is that it was not authored by Laxmi herself, who is not a Marathi speaker, though she has lived in Mumbai for long, but was written by Vaishali Rode, a Marathi journalist to whom Laxmi spoke. The disadvantage of this kind of reportage is that it relies too heavily on the spoken word, and thus risks being rambling and sloppy in structure. Thus, while translating *Mi Hijra, Mi Laxmi*, we found ourselves not merely playing the role of translators, but also of editors, responsible for tightening and 'cleaning up' the original, as it were. The title, on the other hand, posed absolutely no problems to us, the Marathi 'mi' and the English 'me' meaning more or less the same thing. We decided to give the work its present title to retain the flavour of the original title in Marathi. An excerpt from our translation first appeared in the online American journal *Words without Borders*, edited by Rohan Kamicheriyal, and was well received. It is this that encouraged us to translate the entire book. Laxmi had to be tracked down for permission, and I remember nervously meeting her one Sunday morning at no less a place than the Maharashtra chief minister's official residence, Varsha, at Malabar Hill, Mumbai, where she was attending a meeting.

'Do it—you are one of us,' Laxmi said to me, smiling, as I hastened to call my co-translator Joshi in Kopargaon, Maharashtra, where he lives, to ask him to begin work.

R. Raj Rao
2014

WORKS CITED

Revathi, A., *The Truth about Me: A Hijra Life Story*, tr. V. Geetha (New Delhi: Penguin Books India, 2010).

Rushdie, Salman, 'The Half-Woman God', in Negar Akhavi (ed.), *AIDS Sutra: Untold Stories from India* (New Delhi: Random House India, 2008).

Glossary

aadhaar	support, foundation, or base
amanat	safekeeping
aravani	Tamil for a hijra
atithi devo bhavah	Sanskrit for 'The guest is equivalent to god'
bade bhaiya	elder brother
badhai	blessings given by a hijra to a newborn
banda	casual way to address a person
barakhana	feast
besan	chickpea flour
chacha	father's brother
chakka	derogatory word for hijra
chatai	ceremony in which hijras choose their disciples
chatala	initiation rite for a hijra

chawl	large building divided into several separate tenements, offering cheap, basic accommodation to the individuals
chela	disciple
daan	gifts given to a Brahman after the performance of last rites
dadguru	grandmother
dahi handi	earthen pot filled with curd; based on the myth of the mischievous Lord Krishna stealing butter in childhood, this festival, celebrated on Gokul Ashtami, involves men forming a human pyramid and breaking the pot filled with curd that is tied at a height
dai	nurse
dargah	tomb or shrine of a Muslim saint
doctarni	female doctor
Ekla chalo	Bengali for 'Walk alone'; authored by Rabindranath Tagore, this Bengali patriotic song says 'If no one responds to your call, then go your own way alone'
fauji	soldier
Gandharva	singer god whose music is divine

ghagara-choli	long skirt and short-sleeved bodice worn by Indian women, often embroidered and decorated with mirrors
gharana	illustrious family with its own special traditions
gurubhai	fellow disciples of the same guru, hence, like brothers
gutkha	sweetened mixture of chewing tobacco, betel nut, and palm nut, often used as a breath freshener
guttari	last day of the month of Ashadh, as referred to in Maharashtra
haldi-kumkum	initiation ceremony in which turmeric and kumkum are applied on the forehead
haldi-mehndi	ceremony following the castration in which turmeric is applied to the body of the castrated hijra
havildar	soldier or police officer corresponding to a sergeant
hijar	Urdu for hijra
hijra	enuch
hijrakhana	place where hijras live together
janwa	sacred thread ceremony for the Brahmans ceremony

jijaji	brother-in-law
jogjanam	saris given at the time of initiation of a hijra
jogwa	religious devotional song in praise of goddess in which the devotee begs for food and blessings
kathoy	lady boys of Thailand
khwaja sara	Urdu for hijras
kinnar	another name for hijras
koti	effeminate, homosexual men
lavani	genre of music popular in Maharashtra
maike	maternal home
mangalsutra	sacred marital necklace of black beads worn by married women according to Hindu custom
mantra	minister
massi	mother's sister
morcha	organized march or rally
mujra	form of dance originated by tawaifs during the Mughal era; it incorporated elements of the classical Kathak dance onto music or poems
naka	originally a place where tax is levied; a cross road

nani	grandmother
napunsakudu	literally, impotent; this is the Telugu term for hijras
narayan bali	feast on the eleventh day observed after the passing away of a relative
navvari	nine-yard sari
nayak	leader
nirvana	castration of a hijra
nukkad	corner where people gather for gossip
pallu	loose end of a sari
panch	successor of a guru
panga	issue or a fight
parivar	family
parnani	great grandmother
patao	win someone over through sweet talk
pehli nazar	literally, 'At first glance'
purdahguru	great grandmother
qurbani	sacrifice
raas-garba	Gujarati dance in which songs are sung during Navratra festival
reet	christening ceremony for a hijra
saab	sir
sarkari	of that related to the government (sarkar)
sattvic	pure vegetarian food

sutak	period of pollution observed on the death of a relative
tapori	vagabond or rowdy
tawaif	courtesan
thayamma	hijra who performs another hijra's castration
Tijja	this follows the Muslim festival Muharram where many hijras choose their disciples
urs	death anniversary of a Sufi saint
yaar	friend
yaksha	attractive-looking gods from Indian mythology

Foreword to the Marathi Edition

*O*n the occasion of the publication of the Marathi work *Mi Hijra, Mi Laxmi*, I got introduced to Laxmi Tripathi, Gauri, and other hijras. One lived in the limelight, while others groped their way in the darkness of humiliation. During my internship in 1977, and thereafter from 1978 to 1980 when I studied psychiatry, I had met young men who had been traumatized by their sexual orientation. They were sexually attracted to members of their own sex. There was not much communication between these men and women. Mystery and secrecy surrounded their lives. Later, when I met hijras, I was bewildered. They lived such queer, unusual lifestyles. As a student of medicine, I was goaded to learn more about the hijras. Psychology as a discipline was making rapid strides in the understanding of the human mind and the human brain. I was trying to establish a rapport with those who were confused about their sexual orientation. I was convinced that homosexuality was not abnormal. Psychiatry had already taken a positive view about same-sex relationships. Though this was way back in 1973, it took us four decades—1973 to 2013—to understand that homosexuality is not a disease, and is as natural as heterosexuality.

The *Diagnostics and Statistics Manual* of May 2013 does not classify homosexuality as a mental disorder or Gender Identity Disorder. Instead, it regards homosexuality as 'Gender Dysphoria' which is a bitter feeling about one's queer sexuality that results in the fear of humiliation. I sensitized myself towards homosexual people and conducted psychological tests on them. I found them to be in perfect mental and psychological health. What they needed was counselling. They needed to be counselled so that they could overcome the confusion, fear, restlessness, and despair that sometimes drove them to suicide. The parents of homosexual children, who wanted to make them 'normal', also had to be counselled. I encountered intolerant parents who thought that instead of treating their kids, I was brainwashing them (the parents) into accepting their children's sexuality.

Third-gender people regularly came to me to ask for certificates that would enable them to have sex realignment surgery. The tests I conducted on them to prove that they were normal made them impatient. There was the conservative element in the psychiatric profession that still believed that hijras and homosexuals were abnormal persons who needed to be treated. They accused doctors like me of indulging patients who were obviously sick.

In the case of hijras like Laxmi, the genitals are male while the sexual desire they feel is that of women. This is caused by a bungling up of X and Y chromosomes in the human body, resulting in low testosterone levels that make them feel feminine. Their body language, too, is distinctly womanly. Because they do not feel masculine, hijras come to hate their male sexual organs and want to have them surgically removed. They want to have breasts instead of chests, and hormone therapy makes this possible.

In human society, one's sexual organs are supposed to determine one's gender and sexual orientation. We call a human being with a penis and testicles male, and expect him to be attracted to women. We call a human being with a vagina and breasts female, and expect her to be attracted to men. Nature, however, does not always see it in such straightforward terms. Hence, people like Laxmi exist in the world.

Up to the age of four, the behaviour of children does not indicate what their sexual orientation is. At this stage, children accept the sexual identity that adults give them. Between the ages of three and four, children can discriminate between a male and a female child. The majority of them intuitively know that boys will grow up to be fathers and girls' mothers.

Between three-and-a-half to four-and-a-half years, boys are inclined to choose boys as friends, while girls show a preference for girls. The games that the children play can be linked to their gender: boys play rough and tough games, whereas girls play with dolls. Such gender-based difference in the games they play has the sanction of society. Then, between the ages of four and six, the different sexual make up of boys and girls impacts their behaviour, speech, and dress.

By the time he is six years old, a boy who is 'different' from other boys is overcome by anxiety. He begins to loathe himself. At times he might forcibly try to be like other boys, but without success. This continues till teenage, when he comes to terms with the fact that he is effeminate and prefers the company of girls.

Of course, all children who experience these feelings do not become hijras.

In some Indian homes with many boys but without a girl child, a boy may be made to dress and grow his hair like a girl. The phenomenon is social, and does not in itself imply that such a boy is, or will, become homosexual.

Hijras are considered ugly. But when I see Laxmi—tall, sturdy, beautiful, and confident—my stereotypes are automatically destroyed. To hijras, Laxmi is the light at the end of the tunnel. But Laxmi is an exception. Her education, her talent, and the backing she received from her family have given her a good life. Other hijras are not so fortunate. Most of them are thrown out of their homes and are forced to beg on the streets and do sex work. Death alone liberates them from the wretched lives they are compelled to lead. They aspire to be loved, but know that this is only a dream.

People think the hijras themselves are to blame for the way society sees them. They alienate us by the vulgar way in which they walk, talk, dress, and clap. But what else can they do? Will anyone give them jobs that will keep them away from singing, dancing, begging, and prostituting themselves?

The answer is a resounding NO.

PRADEEP PATKAR
2012

Preface to the Marathi Edition

*I*t must have been sometime around the year 1999. I worked with *Mahanagar*, a Mumbai-based newspaper. My husband Pramod worked for the MDACS. Mobile phones were rare then, so even at home we would get landline calls related to office work. One such call that Pramod often got was from Nani.

'This is Nani here. May I speak to Pramodji?'

Though 'nani' means grandmother, a female, the voice on the phone was unmistakably a male voice. I was intrigued. I asked Pramod who Nani was. He told me that Nani was a hijra. Then he proceeded to tell me about Nani, and her work with the DWS.

Shortly afterwards, I read about a hijra conference in the newspapers. I was curious. I had no idea what a hijra conference was. So I thought of asking Nani. I told Pramod to call me when Nani visited his office.

A few days later, Pramod called me. 'Nani and Laxmi are here,' he said. 'If you want to meet them, now is your chance.'

I rushed to the MDACS office at Wadala, Mumbai. I met this guru–chela duo there. The guru, Nani, was middle-aged, while the chela, Laxmi, was in her twenties. They had come to pick up a supply of condoms. I told them I was a reporter and wanted to talk to them about their work. They invited me to accompany them to the DWS office at Govandi. I went, and the visit was hugely illuminating. I saw that Laxmi was no run-of-the-mill hijra.

That was my first encounter with Laxmi, who was elegantly dressed in a white sari. She was tall, slim, and graceful.

Nani, Laxmi, and I became friends. When they called Pramod on official work, they first inquired about me.

My curiosity was aroused. I wanted to know more about the hijras. Pramod told me a little, but that was superficial. I got my big chance when Nikhil Wagle, the editor of *Mahanagar*, asked me to do a story on Laxmi for our Diwali issue. I was happy but unsure. Did I know enough about Laxmi to profile her? I called Laxmi and fixed up an appointment. We met at Barista's Coffee House, Shivaji Park. I told her about the article my editor wanted me to do. She agreed, but was reticent. She did not open up easily. At the end of our meeting, I realized I did not have enough material for an article in our Diwali issue. I gave it a couple more tries before giving up on the project altogether. All I had managed to learn about Laxmi was that she was a graduate and she lived with her parents.

But I could not forget Laxmi. Meanwhile, Pramod quit his job at the MDACS. With that, what little chance I had of bumping into Laxmi was gone forever. Yet, whenever I saw a hijra on the streets, I thought of Laxmi. She had made me see that hijras were no freaks.

One day, as I left my house in the afternoon, I saw a hijra in salwar kameez approaching me. As our paths crossed, she said to me, 'Didi, can you please zip up my top at the back?' It so happened that the zip of her top had come undone. I zipped it up. The hijra gave me a smile and said 'Thanks, Didi' and left. As I looked around, I was aghast to see shopkeepers in the area sniggering at me for fastening a hijra's zip. Their comments made me feel I had done something strange. I had never been in such a situation before.

Much later, when my account of Laxmi's life materialized, not for an article, but for a book, she frequently said to me, 'I tell my hijras that we too are partly responsible for the social stigma that we face. If we mix with people and have a dialogue with them, their perceptions are bound to change.'

How the book came about is interesting. It happened on a rainy day in the year 2009, when I went to Pune to meet Arvind Patkar of Manovikas Publications. The Delhi High Court judgement that read down Section 377 of the Indian Penal Code was just out. There was jubilation in the gay community, which included transgender people like Laxmi. I saw Laxmi on various TV channels, and she spoke with conviction. Patkar turned to me and said, 'Laxmi is a real firebrand.'

I revealed that I knew Laxmi personally. I asked him if he would publish her autobiography, which was my dream project. He said, 'Go ahead. It will be a fascinating work.'

I contacted Laxmi as soon as I got back from Pune. I told her straightaway about the book. She was happy. We decided to meet soon.

I started on the book by downloading stuff on Laxmi from the Internet. I made a blueprint of what her autobiography must include. Pramod pitched in with his suggestions. Then I discussed my outline with Patkar.

But the book could not take off without my having extended sessions with Laxmi herself. When I called her,

I was told that she was ill, and when I called again a week or so later, she was hospitalized. She was diagnosed with pneumonia.

I was put off. Laxmi's sickness, just when I was about to start my work with her, did not augur well. There was nothing I could do but patiently wait for her to get better. When she was finally discharged from the hospital, I went to see her. She was dressed in a skirt and a T-shirt. She had not shaved in the hospital, and I was seeing her sans make-up for the first time. I showed her my blueprint of her autobiography. She offered her suggestions. I got home ready to put pen to paper. I was so excited.

I met Laxmi as and when she found time. Sometimes it would be late in the evening; at other times it would be on holidays. At first, I got the feeling that I was only skimming the surface. I was not probing deep enough. But as time went by, I managed to ferret information out of her regarding her childhood. That helped because I was convinced that the seeds of Laxmi's life lay in her childhood. Laxmi, however, was uncomfortable discussing her childhood. She was traumatized by its memories. Often, as we began talking, she would impulsively end our chat, saying, 'Let us do it tomorrow.' We would plan to have day-long sessions, but she would tire in just an hour. I realized her exhaustion was not physical. It was emotional. She simply did not want to bring the skeletons of her childhood out of the cupboard. I was sorry to hassle her so. At the same time, I felt her story needed to be told.

Laxmi is moody and impetuous. She is also sickly. This slowed my pace of work. I wondered if I was wasting my time, if my book would ever see the light of day.

Even so, I continued interviewing Laxmi. The odds were against me. Her father was diagnosed with cancer, and she was in a state of turmoil. She spent a lot of time attending to him, taking him to the hospital for surgery and chemotherapy. She also frequently went abroad to attend conferences. I, too, was bogged down by office work and home management.

I finally zeroed in on a workable timetable. I would land up at Laxmi's house in Thane at eight in the morning and literally drag her out of bed. After she freshened up and had her morning coffee, we would start working and continue for at least a couple of hours without interruption. We stopped only around noon. This went on for several months, at the end of which I was more or less ready with my first draft. Meeting Laxmi at home helped, for I could see for myself how smoothly she interacted with her family and with some of her chelas. As my notes neared completion, I sometimes took a week off from my office to finalize them. I made sure to jot down everything Laxmi said then and there, so that it did not slip from memory. If there was anything I was not clear about, I paused and got it clarified.

Laxmi's family—comprising her parents, brother, sister, sister-in-law, and nephew—was part of the interview process. They chipped in, telling me things about Laxmi that she herself could not.

In the beginning, Laxmi spoke to me with some hesitation. She probably did not think that I would actually finish and publish my book. But once she saw that I meant business, she stored my number in her mobile phone. A stage came when she would sob as I read out my notes to her. 'Never before have I opened my life to anyone,' she would say. If she liked what I had written, she would make me read it out to her again and again, and insist that others in the family also hear it. She would compliment me and say I knew her better than she knew herself. If I did not meet her for days at a stretch, she would promptly buzz me at 11 a.m., which was early morning for her. 'Aren't you ashamed we haven't met for so long?' she would playfully admonish me. When I apologized and got to her place post-haste, I would find her seated before a large mirror, attending to her make-up. 'My life is like this mirror,' she would say:

As Laxmi's life unfolded before me, I was surprised. Her life overwhelmed me. As we sat in restaurants sipping coffee, I would meet people close to her. One was a friend, another was a son. Her tone varied as she spoke to them. It was as if there was a software installed in her head that programmed her with the appropriate responses, depending on who she spoke to. People respected her. A random banana seller might say to her, 'Sister, why didn't you come for the Ganpati festival yesterday?' Similarly, a random youth might inquire why she was not present at a certain wedding where everyone missed her. Once, soon after her father's death, we went to the post office. The clerk there knew her and said to her, 'Don't worry, madam. We see you very often. Your work will be done, but please sign these papers first.' I could not believe it. I had never seen anyone speak to a hijra that politely. But then I realized that that was because Laxmi herself behaved normally with the world. She did not have a chip on her shoulder. There was so much banter between her and everyone she knew. But she never let it degenerate into loose talk.

That she was a celebrity was evident. I once accompanied her to the passport office, where all the women employees wanted to be photographed with her. Their reason: their kids did not believe that Laxmi graced their office. So they wanted proof. They talked to her about sexual harassment at the workplace and wanted her to be their leader.

On the streets of Thane, Laxmi was a star. But at home, she did not put on airs. She was the dutiful eldest son of her parents and eldest brother of her siblings. Likewise, she was the friend, philosopher, and guide of her chelas.

Laxmi had many boyfriends. But she was circumspect about discussing her love life. If there is one thing her autobiography lacks, it is the details about her romantic and sexual life. In my conversations with her, she never referred to her boyfriends by their real names. She always used false names. 'They're married and with children,' she said. 'Why should I jeopardize their lives by letting the world know that they slept with me?'

She was equally circumspect when talking about her community. Hijras are supposed to keep certain things confidential, she pointed out. She would start talking about her community and then break off midway through a sentence. 'I cannot say anything more,' she would ruefully say. 'There is a binding on me.' The journalist in me tried to probe, but invariably I came up against a wall.

Laxmi's autobiography may shock the conservative society, which has preconceived notions about hijras, about their way of walking, talking, dressing, and clapping. But Laxmi's own language and demeanour contest this. She is cultured to her fingertips.

This book would not have been possible without the help and support of so many people, and I would like to thank all of them individually. I must start with Arvind Patkar of Manovikas Publications, who gave me the green signal to go ahead with my whimsical idea and encouraged me till the very end. I owe a big thank you to my husband Pramod who introduced me to Laxmi and other hijras of the DWS. At home, Pramod and I had many brainstorming sessions about the execution of the book.

Laxmi's parents, her brother Shashi, and sister-in-law Sapna proved immensely helpful and friendly, and without their backing the project would never have gotten off the ground. Likewise, her chelas—Shahin, Kamal, Payal, Muskan, and Annu—kept up my spirits with the piping hot snacks and cups of masala chai they served me as I worked. They also filled in the blanks whenever Laxmi forgot to mention something important that had taken place in her life.

My own friends, Sushil Surve, Shalaka, and Yeshwant Deshmukh, patiently went through several drafts of this book and made valuable suggestions. I am grateful to them. Sunil Karnik often called me to inquire about the progress of my manuscript. Even my school-going son Gandhar stood behind me, as I banged away on my laptop, and suggested improvements.

Then there are my in-laws, Vasanti and Vasant Nigudkar, and my parents, Supriya and Sadanand Rode, who relieved me of household chores and made it possible for me to write my book. My colleagues at *Sakal* often stood in for me when I absented myself from work to spend time with Laxmi.

And how can I not thank Laxmi herself who gave me the permission to make her life public? She stood by me through thick and thin, even though at times we got on each other's nerves and her cavalier attitude infuriated me.

Arvind Patkar and his son Ashish Patkar began typesetting the manuscript as soon as it was handed over to them. The compositor Ganesh Dixit and cover artist Girish Sahasrabudhe worked with commitment. I am thankful to them.

VAISHALI RODE

2012

About the Translators

R. RAJ RAO is a novelist, short-story writer, poet, playwright, biographer, and critic. His iconic novel *The Boyfriend* has been translated into Italian and French, and is soon to be made into a major motion picture. One of India's foremost queer theorists, Rao teaches at the Department of English, University of Pune, Maharashtra.

P.G. JOSHI taught English language and literature at K.J. Somaiya College, Kopargaon, Maharashtra. He wrote his doctoral dissertation on Shashi Deshpande's fiction under the guidance of R. Raj Rao. His book reviews and research articles have appeared in reputed journals and newspapers such as *New Quest*, *BEAM*, *The Indian PEN*, and *The Sunday Times of India*. He has written a few short stories and articles in Marathi as well.